CASPAR HA

AN ACCOUNT

OF

AN INDIVIDUAL KEPT IN A DUNGEON,

SEPARATED FROM ALL COMMUNICATION WITH THE WORLD, FROM EARLY CHILDHOOD TO ABOUT THE AGE OF SEVENTEEN.

Drawn up from Legal Documents.

BY ANSELM VON FEUERBACH,

PRESIDENT OF ONE OF THE BAVARIAN COURTS OF APPEAL, &c.

THIRD EDITION.

WITH A MEMOIR OF THE AUTHOR.

TO WHICH ARE ADDED,

FURTHER INTERESTING DETAILS,

BY

G. F. DAUMER, AND SCHMIDT VON LÜBEC.

LONDON:
SIMPKIN AND MARSHALL.

1834.

Righteous Heaven, who hast permitted
All this wo; what fatal crime
Was by me, e'en at the time
Of my hapless birth committed.
        Sigismund.
    In Caulderon's Life, a Dream.

HODSON, PRINTER, CROSS STREET, HATTON GARDEN.

PREFACE

TO THE SECOND ENGLISH EDITION.

THE interest excited in Germany respecting Caspar Hauser has caused the publication there of several pamphlets relative to his history. Through the kindness and condescension of the Rt. Hon. Earl Stanhope, in directing the Editor's attention to these, he has been enabled to procure one written by Professor Daumer, containing further Details, and a Narrative by Caspar himself; and another by M. Schmidt Von Lübec, consisting of Observations on the Letters which Caspar brought, and conjectures on the subject.

From both these works, many additional particulars have been translated; which, it is presumed, will not only give further interest to the narrative, but will also tend to corroborate its general authenticity.

On this latter point, the pamphlet of Professor Daumer is highly valuable, confirming, as it does, all the facts related by Feuerbach;

and, lest it might be supposed that he had copied these from the latter,—the Professor, in concluding his Preface, states, "In writing this Pamphlet, I could not avail myself of Feuerbach's excellent work on Caspar Hauser, as, when I received it, the printing of mine was completed."

The editor has also the authority of Lord Stanhope, who has adopted this youth, for stating that the account of the leading circumstances of Caspar's case, viz. "the seclusion from the world and from the works of nature, is substantially true."

A Brief Memoir of Feuerbach is given with this edition; which, by shewing the high estimation in which he is held, will enable the reader to form an opinion as to the correctness of his narrative.

The translation has been carefully revised by examination with the German original; and, in those parts of the Appendix which are from the pen of Caspar himself, the style of the original has been closely preserved.

London, Oct. 1833.

TO THE RT. HON. EARL STANHOPE,
&c. &c. &c.

To no one could this Dedication have been addressed with greater propriety than to your Lordship; in whose person Providence has appointed to the youth, without childhood and boyhood, a paternal friend and powerful protector. Beyond the sea, in fair old England, you have prepared for him a secure retreat, until the rising sun of truth shall have dispersed the darkness which still hangs over his mysterious fate; perhaps, in the remainder of his half murdered life, he may yet hope for days, for the sake of which, he will no longer regret his having seen the light of this world. For such a deed, none but the genius of Humanity can recompense you.

In the vast desert of the present times, when the hearts of individuals are more and more shrivelled and parched by the fires of selfish passions, to have met once more with a real man, is one of the most pleasing and indelibly impressive occurrences which have adorned the evening scenery of my life.

With inmost veneration and love,

I am,

Your Lordship's

Most obedient servant,

VON FEUERBACH.

PREFACE.

In offering the following pages to the public, it will be necessary to say but a very few words on the subject of them, or of their distinguished German author and of his translator, in order to show the peculiar claims which they have to the attention of the reader. As to the first, it will be sufficient to state that Caspar Hauser is the individual of whom many persons will recollect to have seen, some years ago, an account in the papers of the day. He was then represented as having been found in Nuremberg, in a state which threw the greatest mystery over his previous life. Hauser was at that time, about sixteen or seventeen years old, and had never learned to speak; and soon showed that he had been shut out during his whole life from all communication with the world. A narrow, dark dungeon, in which he was always obliged to remain in a sitting posture, so that even his bones had assumed a peculiar shape, had been all the space allowed to the unhappy being in this wide world; water and coarse bread, all the food he had ever tasted; a shirt, all his clothing; and now and then stripes, inflicted by the unseen hand of his fiendish keeper, when he happened to make a noise—all he knew of any being besides himself. He was but just allowed to vegetate—and what a wretched vegetation in his forlorn condition!

Great pains, as the reader will see, have been taken, without success, to raise the veil of mystery hanging over this foul transaction, continued even by an attempt to murder the youth, when it was falsely reported in the newspapers, that he was occupied in writing his biography. But the great attention which was thus directed to him, has, though unsuccessful as to the detection of the perpetrators of the crime, not been without its fruits; and it may be easily imagined, how interesting must be a faithful account, like the following, of the process of physical and intellectual acclimatisation to life, if we may be allowed to use this expression, which a youth must undergo to fit him for society—for life and light, after his soul, intellect, and body had been left from his birth dormant and undeveloped—abandoned to perfect solitude. Light had never shone upon this being, neither on his eye, nor on his soul; and when he emerged from his lonesome darkness, he was like a new-born child, in respect to all which must be acquired by experience; whilst the instruments for acquiring that experience, the natural faculties, of course, differed from those of a child so far as they are affected by the mere age or growth of the individual. Thus he presented an opportunity for observation of the highest interest to the philosopher, the moralist, the religious teacher, the physiologist, and the physician — an opportunity which must be as rare as the crime which has afforded it.

Uncommonly attractive, however, as the account of this interesting individual must prove to every reflecting reader, whether he considers particularly the moral, the intellectual, or the physical condition of the being described, its value is much enhanced to the lawyer, by the legal point of view in which its philosophical and eminent author, in one part of the work, examines his subject, as constituting a species of crime never yet duly treated by any code of legislation — a view, forcibly expressed in the title of the German original, which is thus, *Kaspar Hauser. Beispiel eines Verbrechens am Seelenleben des Menschen**, which, literally translated, would be, K. H. An Instance of a Crime against the Life of the Soul (the Development of all its intellectual, moral, and immortal parts) of Man. We are sorry not to be able to preserve this title in English; the reasons for which, however, are obvious to the greater part of our legal readers. M. Von Feuerbach is well known as one of the most distinguished jurists of the age, both for his extensive learning and the philosophical acuteness displayed in his numerous works, chiefly on penal law. He, moreover, drew up the penal code of Bavaria, and is at this time president of one of the Bavarian courts of appeal. Nothing indifferent can come from his pen, nothing

* Anspach, 1832

doubtful be guaranteed by his name: and it is hardly necessary to add, that the whole account is founded on official documents, wherever it pretends to give positive facts; and that the only duty of those who offer a work of so eminent an author of another country to the public, is to give an exact translation.

In conclusion, we would mention, that the translator of this work is the same gentleman who has done himself so much credit by an English version of M. Cousin's History of Philosophy*; a task of no common difficulty, and yet so successfully performed as to be a pledge for the faithful execution of the present work.

* Introduction to the History of Philosophy by Victor Cousin, Professor of Philosophy. Translated from the French by Hennin Gottfried Linberg. Boston, 1832. London, O. Rich.

Nov. 1832.

BRIEF MEMOIR

OF

M. VON FEUERBACH.

"FEUERBACH, PAUL JOHN ANSELM VON, since 1821, royal Bavarian acting Counsellor of State; since 1817, President of the court of Appeal of the circle of Rezat, member of several orders, and of the Law Commission at St. Petersburg, &c., was born November 14, 1775, and educated at Frankfort on the Maine, where his father, a lawyer, resided. He studied the Greek and Roman classics in the Gymnasium at that place; and commenced the study of philosopy and law at Jena, in 1792. The study of the works of Kant, Locke, Hume, Tetens, Lambert, &c., led him to investigations of the foundation, of legal principles. With his mind thus strengthened by philosophical studies, he turned his attention to positive law. In 1798, he wrote his *Anti Hobbes;* and, by an Essay on High Treason, and a Treatise on the Design of Punishment, first made his appearance among the writers on criminal law. He was also highly popular as teacher of law at Jena, 1799. By the Revision of the Fundamental Principles of Criminal Law, 2 vols., 1799, and by the Library of Criminal Law, edited by him, with Grolman and Almendingen, he prepared the way for the revision of the penal laws, which he executed systematically in his Manual of the Private Criminal Law of Germany (Giessen, 1801—9, nearly all written anew in the edition of 1826). By this work he placed himself at the head of the new school of criminal writers, called *Rigorists*, who allow no discretion to the judge, but confine him to a strict administration of the law, as set down in the codes and statutes. In 1801, Feuerbach received an ordinary professorship at Jena; in 1802, he accepted an invitation to Kiel, where he published, at the suggestion of a learned Bavarian, " A Review of the Plan of Kleinschrod, for a Penal Code, adapted to the Electoral Palatine Bavarian States," 3 vols., 1804. In 1804 he was invited to Landshut, being the first Protestant and foreigner who received this honour from the superintendents of a Bavarian university, and was commissioned to prepare a plan for a Bavarian penal code. The entire reform of the penal code of Bavaria commenced in 1806, with the abolition of torture, and the regulation of the proceedings against prisoners refusing to plead, an ordinance drawn up by Feuerbach himself. The new penal code for the kingdom of Bavaria, which he had drawn up, received the royal sanction May 16, 1813, after a previous examination and some alterations. This work has been taken as a basis for the new codes in Weimar, Würtemberg, and other states. In the duchy of Oldenburg, it was adopted entirely, and was afterwards translated into Swedish. At the same time, 1807, Feuerbach was commanded by the king to adapt the *Code Napoleon,* as a general civil code, to the situation of the kingdom of Bavaria; which, however, has never gone into operation. Among the works published at that time, by Feuerbach, are, Remarkable Criminal Cases, 2 vols., 1808—11 *; *Themis,* or Con-

* In a review of this work, in the Law Magazine, No. 22,

tributions to Legislation, 1812; and Observations on Trial by Jury, Landshut, 1812. Feuerbach rejected the French jury; and many works were written both for and against his views. In his work on the Publicity of Judicial Proceedings, Giessen, 1821, he has expressed many of his opinions more explicitly, and shewn how a public judicial process, adapted to the circumstances of Germany, might combine oral and written forms.

"At the restoration of German independence, 1813, Feuerbach displayed his patriotism and public spirit by several publications; such as, On German Freedom, and the Representation of the German People, Leipsic, 1814. About this time, the king appointed him second president of the Court of Appeal in Bamberg. Feuerbach afterwards travelled into foreign countries, and lived at Munich, devoted to letters, until March 1817, when he was ap-

April 1833, M. Von Feuerbach is mentioned in the following terms: " Besides being a highly distinguished judge, he has long ranked as one of the most learned and enlightened cultivators of criminal jurisprudence, scientifically considered, in the world."

pointed first president of the Court of Appeal, of the circle of Rezat, at Anspach.

" This unwearied jurist and scholar occupied his leisure moments with a poetical translation and commentary of the Indian poem, *Gita Gowinda*. In the spring and summer of 1821, he visited Paris, Brussels, and the Rhenish Provinces, by the direction of the king, for the purpose of studying the judicial systems in those places; an account of which he has given in his learned work on the Judicial System and Process in France, Giessen, 1825; in which he has explained the minutest details with clearness and accuracy. The life of this able man entitles him to a place not merely in the annals of literature, but likewise in the history of legislation; and Feuerbach will always be spoken of with veneration, like Beccaria. Some of his works have gone through many editions."—*Encyclopædia Americana, Vol. V.*

The last work which proceeded from the pen of M. Feuerbach was "Caspar Hauser." He died at Frankfort in the summer of 1833.

CASPAR HAUSER.

CHAPTER 1.

WHITMONDAY is at Nuremberg a day of great festivity; when most of its inhabitants sally forth from the city, and disperse themselves in the neighbouring country and villages. The appearance of the city, which, in consequence of the present scantiness of its population, is very straggling, reminds us on such occasions, and particularly in fine spring weather, rather of an enchanted city in the desert, than of an active, bustling, manufacturing town; and many secret deeds may, in situations remote from its centre, then be done publicly, without ceasing to be secret.

It was on Whitmonday, the 26th of May, 1828, between four and five o'clock in the evening, that the following occurrence took place.

A citizen who lived at Unschlitt place, near the small and little-frequented Haller-gate, was still loitering before his door, about to proceed upon his intended ramble through the New-gate, when, looking around him, he remarked at a little distance a young man in a peasant's dress, who was standing in a very singular posture, and, like an intoxicated person, was endeavouring to move forward, without being fully able either to stand upright or to govern the movements of his legs. The citizen approached the stranger, who held out to him a letter directed "To his honour the Captain of the 4th Esgataron of the Shwolishay regiment, Nuremberg." As the Captain, apparently referred to, lived near the New-gate, the citizen took the strange youth along with him to the guard-room, whence the latter was conducted to the dwelling of Captain von. W. who, at that time, commanded the 4th squadron of the 6th regiment of Light Horse (Chevaux legers), and who lived in the neighbourhood.* The stranger advanced towards

* The depositions concerning what passed while Caspar and the above mentioned citizen were on their way from Unschlitt place to the guard-room and thence to Captain von W———'s dwelling, are so defective, so unsatisfactory, and withal so apocryphal, that I have thought proper to reduce their contents within a very narrow compass. Thus, for instance, the citizen before mentioned has deposed, that, after many attempts to enter into conversation with Caspar, and after having asked him several questions, he at length perceived that Caspar neither knew nor had the least conception of what he meant, and that he therefore ceased to speak

the captain's servant who opened the door, with his hat on his head and the letter in his hand, with the following words: " Ae sechtene möcht ih waehn, wie mei Votta waehn is." The servant asked him what he wanted? who he was? whence he came? But the stranger appeared to understand none of these questions; and his only reply was a repetition of the words, " Ae sechtene möcht ih waehn, wie mei Votta waehn is;" or, " Woas nit." He

to him. From this circumstance it would appear, that Caspar's conduct towards him was the same as it was in the evening, at Captain von W——'s, and afterwards at the guard-room; and as it continued to be for several days and weeks in succession. Nevertheless the same citizen has also stated, that Caspar had replied to the question, whence he came? " From Regensburg." And also, that when they came to the New-gate, Caspar had said; " That has just been built since they call it the New-gate," &c. That witness fully believes he heard such expressions appears to me to be as certain, as that Caspar never said any such thing. This is fully proved by all that follows; for it is highly probable that the words which Caspar repeatedly uttered, "Reuta waehn wie mein Votta waehn is," may have thus been understood by his conductor, who would scarcely have paid much attention to the words of such a simpleton as he conceived him to be. But, upon the whole, the official documents, showing the proceedings of the police on this occasion, prove, that they have been so irregular, that the depositions taken contain so many contradictions, that the witnesses have been so slightly examined, and that many of their assertions contained anachronisms which are so very palpable; that these documents cannot, without much caution, be admitted as genuine sources of historical truth.

was, as the captain's servant declared in his deposition, so much fatigued that he could scarcely be said to walk, but rather to stagger. Weeping, and with the expression of excessive pain, he pointed to his feet, which were sinking under him; and he appeared to be suffering from hunger and thirst. A small piece of meat was handed to him; but scarcely had the first morsel touched his lips, when he shuddered, the muscles of his face were seized with convulsive spasms, and, with visible horror, he spit it out. He showed the same marks of aversion when a glass of beer was brought to him and he had tasted a few drops of it. A bit of bread and a glass of fresh water he swallowed greedily and with extreme satisfaction. In the meantime, all attempts to gain any information respecting his person or his arrival were altogether fruitless. He seemed to hear without understanding, to see without perceiving, and to move his feet without knowing how to use them for the purpose of walking. His language consisted mostly of tears, moans, and unintelligible sounds, or of the words, which he frequently repeated: "Reuta wähn, wie mei Votta wähn is." In the captain's house, he was taken for a kind of savage, and, in expectation of the captain's return, he was conducted to the stable, where he immediately stretched himself on the straw, and fell into a profound sleep.

He had already slept for some hours, when the captain returned and went directly to his stable, in order to see the human savage of whom his children, at his first entrance, had related so many strange things. He still lay in the deepest sleep. Attempts were made to awaken him; he was jogged, he was shaken and thumped, but all to no purpose. They raised him from the ground, and endeavoured to place him on his feet; but he still continued to sleep, and seemed, like a person apparently dead, to be distinguishable from one who is really so only by his vital heat. At length, after many troublesome and painful experiments upon the sleeper's power of feeling, he opened his eyes, awoke, gazed at the bright colors of the captain's glittering uniform, which he seemed to regard with childish satisfaction, and then groaned out his "Reuta, &c." Captain von W—— knew nothing of the stranger, nor could he learn anything relating to him from the letter which he had brought. And as nothing could be got out of him by questioning, but, "Reuta wähn," &c., or "Woas nit;" all that remained to be done, was, to leave the solution of this riddle, and the care of the stranger's person, to the city police. He was accordingly sent forthwith to the police office.

At about eight o'clock in the evening his journey thither, which, in his situation, was a course of martyrdom, was accomplished. In the guard-room, besides some of the inferior magistrates, several soldiers of the police were present. All of them regarded the strange lad as a most extraordinary phenomenon. Nor was it easy to decide to which of the common forms of police business his case appertained. The common official questions, What is your name? what is your business? whence came you? for what purpose are you come? where is your passport? and the like, were here of no avail. "Ae Reuta waehn wie mei Votta waehn is;" or, "Woas nit;" or, which he also often repeated in a lamentable tone, "Hoam weissa!" were the only words which, on the most diverse occasions, he uttered.*

He appeared neither to know nor to suspect where he was. He betrayed neither fear, nor astonishment, nor confusion; he rather showed an almost brutish dulness, which either leaves external objects entirely unnoticed, or stares

---

* To these expressions, and particularly, " Reuta waehn," &c. he attached, as was afterwards discovered, no particular meaning. They were only sounds, which had been taught him like a parrot, and which he uttered as the common expressions of all his ideas, sensations, and desires.

at them without thought, and suffers them to pass without being affected by them. His tears and whimpering, while he was always pointing to his tottering feet, and his awkward and, at the same time, childish demeanour, soon excited the compassion of all who were present. A soldier brought him a piece of meat and a glass of beer; but, as at the house of Captain von W———, he rejected both with abhorrence, and ate only bread with fresh water. Another person gave him a piece of coin. At this he showed the joy of a little child; played with it; and by several times crying, "Ross, ross" [horse, horse], as well as by certain motions of his hands, he seemed to express his wish to hang this coin about the neck of some horse. His whole conduct and demeanor seemed to be that of a child scarcely two or three years old, with the body of a young man.

The only difference of opinion that seemed to exist among the greater part of these police men, was, whether he should be considered as an idiot or madman, or as a kind of savage. One or two of them expressed, however, a doubt, whether, under the appearance of this boy, some cunning deceiver might not possibly be concealed. This suspicion received no small degree of confirmation from the following circumstance. Some person thought of trying whether he could write; and handing him a pen with ink, laid a sheet of paper before him with an intimation that he should write. This appeared to give him pleasure; he took the pen, by no means awkwardly, between his fingers, and wrote, to the astonishment of all who were present, in legible characters, the name, *Kaspar Hauser*.

He was now told to add also the name of the place whence he came. But he did nothing more than occasionally groan out his " Reuta waehn," &c. his " Hoam weissa," and his " Woas nit."

As nothing more could be done for the present, he was delivered to a servant of the police, who conducted him to the tower at the Vestner-gate, which is used as a place of confinement for rogues and vagabonds, &c. Upon this comparatively short way he sank down groaning at almost every step, if, indeed, his groping movements may be called steps. Having reached the small apartment in which, together with another prisoner of the police, he was confined, he sank down immediately upon his straw bed, in a deep sleep.

CHAPTER II.

CASPAR HAUSER—the name which he has hitherto retained—wore upon his head, when he came to Nuremberg, a round and rather coarse felt hat, shaped like those worn in cities, lined with yellow silk, and bound with red leather, inside of which a picture of the city of Munich, half scratched out, was still visible. The toes of his naked feet peeped forth from a pair of high heeled boots, shod with iron shoes and nails, which were much torn and did not fit him. Around his neck was tied a black silk neckcloth. Over a coarse shirt*, and a half faded red spotted stuff waistcoat, he wore a sort of jacket, such as is commonly worn by country people, and is called janker or schalk, but which, as was afterwards proved by a more minute inspection of it, and by the declaration of competent

---

* Which imprudently, together with the boots, was, as was asserted, on account of their bad condition, thrown away very soon after this occurence took place. So little attention was paid to things which, in point of circumstantial evidence, might have become highly important.

judges, was not originally cut out by the tailor for a peasant's jacket. It had, as appears also from the shape of its cape, formerly been a frock coat, of which the skirts had been cut off and the upper part sewed up with coarse stitches by a hand unaccustomed to tailor's work. Also the pantaloons, which were made of gray cloth of a somewhat finer quality, and which, like overalls for riding, were lined between the legs with the same cloth, seemed originally to have belonged to some footman, groom, forester, or some such person, rather than to a peasant. Caspar wore a white handkerchief with red crossed stripes, marked in red with the initials K. H. Besides some blue and white figured rags, a key of German manufacture, and a paper of gold sand—which no one surely would look for in a peasant's cottage—there were found in his pocket a small horn rosary, and a tolerably large store of spiritual wealth, viz., besides manuscript Catholic prayers, several printed spiritual publications, such as, in the south of Germany, and particularly at places to which pilgrims resort, are commonly offered in exchange for good money to the faithful multitude. In some, the places where they were printed were not named. Others appeared to have been printed at Altottingen, Burghausen, Salsburg, and Prague. Their edifying titles were, for instance, "Spiritual Sentinel," — "Spiritual Forget-me-not," — "A very powerful Prayer by virtue of which one may participate in the benefits of all holy Masses," &c., — "Prayer to the holy Guardian Angel," — "Prayer to the holy Blood," &c. One of these precious little spiritual works, entitled "The Art of regaining lost Time and Years misspent," (without mentioning the year of publication,) seems to contain a scoffing allusion to the life which this youth, according to what he afterwards related, had hitherto led. Judging from these spiritual donations, there can be no doubt, that the hands concerned in this transaction were not exclusively secular. The letter addressed, without naming him, to the Captain of the fourth squadron of the sixth regiment of Light Horse, which Caspar held in his hand when he first appeared in Nuremberg, runs as follows*:

* This letter agrees, in the German original, literally with the manuscript alluded to; which, from its style and orthography, appears evidently to have been intended to pass for the production of some ignorant peasant. No attempt has been made by the translator to retain, in this respect, its original character. It has been simply translated into plain English according to what appeared to be the most obvious signification of the words, whose meaning however is not in all its parts perfectly intelligible.

"From a place, near the Bavarian frontier which shall be nameless, 1828.

"HIGH AND WELL-BORN CAPTAIN!

"I send you a boy who wishes faithfully to serve his king. This boy was left in my house the 7th day of October, 1812; and I am myself a poor day-labourer, who have also ten children, and have enough to do to maintain my own family. The mother of the child only put him in my house for the sake of having him brought up. But I have never been able to discover who his mother is; nor have I ever given information to the provincial court that such a child was placed in my house. I thought I ought to receive him as my son. I have given him a Christian education; and since 1812 I have never suffered him to take a single step out of my house. So that no one knows where he was brought up. Nor does he know either the name of my house or where it is. You may ask him but he cannot tell you. I have already taught him to read and write, and he writes my hand-writing exactly as I do. And when we asked him what he would be, he said he would be one of the Light Horse, as his father was. If he had had parents different to what he has, he would have become a learned lad. If you shew him anything, he learns it immediately. I have only shown him the way to Neumark, whence he was to go to you. I told him that when he had become a soldier, I should come to take him home, or I should lose my head. Good Mr. Captain, you need not try him; he does not know the place where I am. I took him away in the middle of the night, and he knows not the way home.

"I am your most obedient servant. I do not sign my name, for I might be punished. He has not a kreutzer of money; because I have none myself. If you do not keep him, you may kill him, or hang him up in the chimney."

With this letter, which was written in German characters, the following note, written in Latin, but evidently by the same hand, was enclosed:

"The child is already baptized. You must give him a surname yourself. You must educate the child: His father was one of the Light Horse. When he is seventeen years old send him to Nuremberg to the sixth regiment of Light Horse, for there his father also was. I ask for his education until he is seventeen years old. He was born the 30th April, 1812. I am a poor girl and cannot support him. His father is dead."

Caspar Hauser* was, when he appeared at Nuremberg, four feet nine inches in height, and about from sixteen to seventeen years old. His chin and lips were very thinly covered with down : the wisdom-teeth, as they are called, were yet wanting ; nor did they make their appearance before the year 1831. His light brown hair, which was very fine and curled in ringlets, was cut according to the fashion of peasants. The structure of his body, which was stout and broad-shouldered, showed perfect symmetry without any visible defect. His skin was fine and very fair; his complexion was not florid, but neither was it of a sickly hue ; his limbs were delicately made ; his small hands were beautifully formed ; and his feet, which showed no marks of ever before having been confined or pressed by a shoe, were equally so. The soles of his feet, which were without any horny skin, were as soft as the palms of his hands ; and they were covered all over with fresh bloody blisters, the marks of which were some months later still visible. Both his arms showed the scars of innoculation ; and on his right arm, a wound still

---

* The following description of his person is not taken from the records of the police, where it was not to be found ; but from my own observations and from the written notes of persons on whom full reliance may be placed.

covered with a fresh scab was observable, which, as Caspar afterwards related, was occasioned by a blow given him with a stick or a piece of wood by the man " with whom he had always been," because he once had made too much noise. His face was at that time very vulgar: when in a state of tranquillity it was almost without any expression; and its lower features, being somewhat prominent, gave him a brutish appearance. The staring look of his blue but clear and bright eyes had also an expression of brutish obtuseness.* The formation of his face altered in a few months almost entirely; his countenance gained expression and animation, the prominent lower features of his face receded more and more, and his earlier physiognomy could scarcely any longer be recognized. His weeping was at first only an ugly contortion of his mouth; but, if any thing pleasant affected his mind, a lovely, smiling, heart-winning sweetness diffused over all his features the irresistible charm that lies concealed in the joy of an innocent child. He

* The author expressed at that time his wish that Caspar's picture might be taken by a skilful portrait painter; because he felt assured that his features would soon alter. His wish was not gratified, but his prediction was very soon fulfilled.

N.B. The portrait prefixed to this edition is taken from the one attached to an edition of Feuerbach's work, since printed at Altona.

scarcely knew at all how to use his hands and fingers. He stretched his fingers out stiff and straight and far asunder, with the exception of his first finger and thumb, whose tips he commonly held together, so as to form a circle. Where others applied but a few fingers he used his whole hand in the most uncouth and awkward manner imaginable. His gait, like that of an infant making its first essays in leading-strings, was, properly speaking, not a walk, but rather a waddling, tottering, groping of his way—a painful medium between the motion of falling and the endeavour to stand upright. In attempting to walk, instead of first treading firmly on his heels, he placed his heels and the balls of his feet at once to the ground, and raising both feet simultaneously with an inclination of the upper part of his body, he stumbled slowly and heavily forward with out-stretched arms, which he seemed to use as balance poles. The slightest impediment in his way, caused him often, in his little chamber, to fall flat on the floor. For a long time after his arrival he could not go up or down stairs without assistance. And even now, it is impossible for him to stand on one foot, and to raise or bend, or stretch the other, without falling down. The following results of a medical examination of the body of Caspar

Hauser, made by order of a court of justice in the year 1830, furnish highly interesting data which throw much light upon the circumstances of his life.

"The knee," says Dr. Osterhausen in his report, "exhibits a remarkable deviation from the usual formation. In the natural structure of the part, the patella or kneepan forms a prominence anteriorly during the extension of the leg. But in Hauser it lay in a considerable depression. In a limb naturally formed, the four extensor muscles of the leg, the vastus externus and the vastus internus, the rectus femoris and the crureus, are attached by a common tendon to a protuberance of the tibia or shin-bone, after having formed an intimate connexion with the kneepan. But in Hauser the tendon was divided; and the two tendons of the external and internal vasti muscles proceeded separately down the leg to the outer and inner sides of the tubercle of the tibia, and were inserted below the tubercle into this bone. Between these two tendons lay the patella. This unusual formation of the part, together with a remarkable development of the two tendons, occasioned the depression in which the patella was situated. When Hauser sits down, with the thigh and leg extended horizontally on the floor, the back forms a right angle with the flexure of the thigh, and the knee-joint lies extended so close to the floor, that not the smallest hollow is perceptible in the ham. A common playing card could scarcely be thrust between the ham and the floor."

CHAPTER III.

The surprise occasioned by Caspar Hauser's first appearance, soon settled down into the form of a dark and horrid enigma, to explain which, various conjectures were resorted to. By no means an idiot or a madman, he was so mild, so obedient, and so good-natured, that no one could be tempted to regard this stranger as a savage, or as a child grown up among the wild beasts of the forest. And yet he was so entirely destitute of words and conceptions, he was so totally unacquainted with the most common objects and daily occurrences of nature, and he showed so great an indifference, nay, such an abhorrence, to all the usual customs, conveniences, and necessaries of life; and at the same time he exhibited such extraordinary peculiarities in all the characteristics of his mental, moral, and physical existence, as seemed to leave us no other choice, than either to regard him as the inhabitant of some other planet, miraculously transferred to the earth, or as one who (like the man whom Plato supposes) had been born and bred under ground, and who, now that he had arrived at the age of maturity, had, for the first time, ascended to the surface of the earth, and beheld the light of the sun.

Caspar showed continually the greatest aversion to all kinds of meat and drink, excepting dry bread and water. Without swallowing or even tasting them, the very smell of most kinds of our common food was sufficient to make him shudder, or to affect him still more disagreeably. The least drop of wine, of coffee, or the like, mixed clandestinely with his water, occasioned him cold sweats, or caused him to be seized with vomiting or violent headache.*

A certain person made, somewhere, the attempt to force some brandy upon him on pretence that it was water; scarcely was the

* It is much to be regretted, that in the whole city of Nuremberg not a single individual was to be found who possessed scientific curiosity sufficient to induce him to make this youth the subject of physiological inquiries. Even the chemical analysis of the saliva, or other substances ejected by this young man, who had been solely fed on bread and water, might alone have furnished many not unimportant scientific results; which would at the same time have verified, as it were with intuitive certainty, the highly important juridical fact, that Caspar had been really fed on no other food. But at the time when the judicial authorities, after many fruitless endeavours on their part, were at length placed in a proper situation to enter into the examination of Hauser's case, every opportunity of making amends for what had been lost by such omissions had long passed by.

glass brought to his lips ere he turned pale, sank down, and would have fallen backward against a glass door, had he not been instantly supported. Once when the prison-keeper had prevailed upon him to take some coffee in his mouth, although he could scarcely have swallowed a single drop of it, his bowels were in consequence thereof repeatedly affected. A few drops of beer made from malted wheat, though much diluted with water, gave him a violent pain in his stomach, accompanied with so great a heat that he was all over dripping with perspiration; which was succeeded by an ague attended with headache and violent eructations. Even milk, whether boiled or fresh, was unpalatable to him, and caused him disgusting belchings. Some meat was once concealed in his bread; he smelt it immediately, and expressed a great aversion to it, but was nevertheless prevailed upon to eat it; he however afterwards felt extremely ill in consequence of having done so. During the night, which, with him, commenced regularly with the setting, and ended with the rising, of the sun, he lay upon his straw bed; in the day time he sat upon the floor with his legs stretched out straight before him. When, in the earlier days, he for the first time saw a lighted candle placed before him, he was so delighted with the shining flame, that he unsuspectingly put his fingers into it; but soon drew them back, crying out and weeping. Feigned cuts and thrusts were made at him with a naked sabre, in order to try what might be their effect upon him; but he remained immoveable, without even winking; nor did he seem to harbour the least suspicion that any harm could thus be done to him.* When a looking-glass was once held before him, he caught at his own reflected image, and then looked behind it to find the person whom he supposed to be concealed there. Like a little child, he endeavoured to lay hold of every glittering object that he saw; and when he could not reach it, or when he was forbidden to touch it, he cried. Some days after his arrival, Caspar was conducted, under the escort of two policemen, around the city, in order to discover whether he could recognize the gate through which he had entered. But, as might have been foreseen, he knew not how to distinguish the one from the other; and, upon the whole, he appeared to take not the least notice of what was passing before his eyes. When objects were brought more than ordi-

* It is even said that, by way of an amusing experiment, a pistol, or some other piece of fire arms, was once discharged at him.

narily near to him, he gazed at them with a stupid look, which, only in particular instances, was expressive of curiosity and astonishment. He was in possession of only two words which he occasionally used for the purpose of designating living creatures. Whatever appeared to him in a human form he called, without any distinction of sex or age, "Bua;" and to every animal that he met with, whether quadruped or biped, dog, cat, goose, or fowl, he gave the name of "ross" (horse). If such horses were *white* he appeared to be pleased; *black* animals were regarded by him with aversion and fear. A black hen, once advancing towards him, put him in great fear; he cried out, and, though his feet refused to perform their office, he made every effort to run away from her.

Not only his mind, but some of his senses appeared at first to be in a state of torpor, and to open but gradually to the perception of external objects. It was not till the lapse of several days that he began to notice the striking of the steeple clock, and the ringing of the bells. This threw him into the greatest astonishment, which, at first, was expressed only by his listening looks and by certain spasmodic motions of his countenance; but it was soon succeeded by a stare of benumbed meditation. Some weeks afterwards the nuptial procession of a peasant passed by the tower with a band of music, close under his window. He suddenly stood listening, motionless as a statue; his countenance appeared to be transfigured, and his eyes, as it were, to radiate his ecstasy; his ears and eyes seemed continually to follow the movements of the sounds as they receded more and more; and they had long ceased to be audible, while he still continued immoveably fixed in a listening posture, as if unwilling to lose the last vibrations of these, to him, celestial notes, or as if his soul had followed them, and left its body behind it, in torpid insensibility. Certainly not by way of making any very judicious trial of Caspar's musical taste, this being, whose extraordinary nervous excitability was already sufficiently apparent, was once, at a military parade, placed very near to the great regimental drum. He was so powerfully affected by its first sounds, as to be immediately thrown into convulsions, which rendered his instantaneous removal necessary.

Among the many remarkable phenomena which appeared in Caspar's conduct, it was soon observed that the idea of *horses*, and particularly of *wooden horses*, was one which, in his eyes, must have acquired no small degree of importance. The word "Ross" (*horse*) appeared in his dictionary, which contained scarcely half a dozen words, to fill the greatest space. This word he pronounced on the most diverse occasions, more frequently than any other, and often indeed with tears in his eyes, and with a plaintive, beseeching tone of voice, which seemed to express a longing for some particular horse. Whenever any trifle, as, for instance, a glittering coin, a ribbon, a little picture, &c., was given to him, he cried, "Ross! Ross!" and notified by his looks and motions his wish to hang all these pretty things upon a horse. Caspar, who—not indeed to any great advantage of his mental development, or to the making of such accurate observations on his peculiarities as the rarity of such a phenomenon rendered desirable—was daily conducted to the guard-room of the police, in the noise and bustle of which he commonly spent a great portion of the day, became there as it were domesticated, and gained the good-will and affection of all its constant attendants. The words, "Ross! Ross!" which, here also, he so often repeated, suggested to one of the police soldiers, who had always taken the most notice of this singular amalgamation of adolescence and childhood, the idea of bringing to him, at the guard-room, a toy of a wooden horse.

Caspar, who had hitherto, on almost all occasions, shewed the greatest insensibility and indifference, and who generally seemed much dejected, appeared now to be, as it were, suddenly transformed, and conducted himself as if he had found in this little horse an old and long desired friend. Without noisy demonstrations of joy, but with a countenance smiling in his tears, he immediately seated himself on the floor by the side of the horse, stroked it, patted it, kept his eyes immoveably fixed upon it, and endeavoured to hang upon it all the variegated, glittering, and tinkling trifles which the benevolence of those about him had presented to him. Now only that he could decorate his little horse with them, did all these things appear to have acquired their true value. When the hour arrived at which he was to leave the police guard room, he endeavoured to lift up the horse, in order to take it along with him; and he wept bitterly when he found that his arms and legs were so weak that he could not lift his favourite over the threshold of the door.* Whenever he

* He was for a long time extremely weak in his arms as well as in his feet. It was not before the month of September, 1828, after he had already commenced to eat meat, that his strength was, by continued exercise, so far increased, as to enable him to lift a weight of twenty-five pounds with both his hands, a little way from the ground.

afterwards returned to the guard-room, he immediately placed himself on the floor by the side of his dear little horse, without paying the least attention to the people who were about him. "For hours together," said one of the police soldiers in the declaration which he afterwards made before the police court, " has Caspar sat playing with his horse by the stove, without attending in the least to anything that passed around him or by his side."

But also in the tower, in his small chamber and sitting room, he was soon supplied not only with one but with several horses. These horses were henceforward, when he was at home, his constant companions and playmates, which he never suffered to be removed from his side, of which he never lost sight, and with which—as could be observed through a concealed opening made in the door—he continually employed himself. Every day, every hour, resembled the other in this, that all of them were passed by Caspar sitting on the floor by the side of his horses, with his legs stretched out before him, and continually employed in ornamenting them one way or another, with ribbons and strings, or with bits of coloured paper; sometimes bedecking them with coins, bells, and spangles, and sometimes appearing to be immersed in thinking how this decoration might be varied by successively placing these articles in different positions. He also often dragged his horses backwards and forwards by his side, without changing his place or altering his position; yet this was done silently and very carefully, for fear, as he afterwards said, that the rolling of the wheels might make a noise and he might be beaten for it. He never ate his bread without first holding every morsel of it to the mouth of some one of his horses; nor did he ever drink water without first dipping their mouths in it, which he afterwards carefully wiped off. One of the horses was of plaster of Paris, and its mouth was consequently very soon softened. He could not conceive how this happened; as he perceived that the mouths of his other horses, although they also were immersed in water, remain unaltered. The prison-keeper, to whom, with tears in his eyes, he shewed the misfortune that had befallen his plaster horse, comforted him by insinuating that "this horse did not like to drink water." In consequence of this information he ceased to water it, as he believed that the horse, by this visible deformity of his mouth, indicated his dislike to water. The prison-keeper, who saw what pains Caspar took to feed his horses with his bread, endeavoured to make him understand that these horses could not eat. But Caspar thought he had sufficiently refuted him by pointing to the crumbs which stuck to their mouths. One of his horses had a bridle in its mouth, which was wide open; hence he also made a bridle of gold spangles joined together for his other horse; and he took great pains to induce it to open its mouth and to let him place the bridle in it; an attempt in which he persisted for two whole days with unwearied perseverance. Having once fallen asleep on a rocking-horse, he fell down and squeezed his finger; upon which he complained that the horse had bitten him. As he was once dragging one of his horses over the floor, its hind feet having got into a hole, it reared up. At this occurrence he expressed the most lively satisfaction; he afterwards frequently repeated a spectacle which appeared to him so very remarkable, and he treated all his visitors with a sight of it. When the prison-keeper afterwards expressed his displeasure at his always showing the same thing to every body, he ceased indeed to do so, but he cried at his being no longer permitted to show his rearing horse. Once, when in rearing, this horse fell down, he ran to it with precipitate tenderness, and expressed his sorrow that it had hurt itself. But he was quite inconsolable when the prison-keeper once drove a nail into one of his horses.

From this, as well as from many other circumstances, it may well be supposed, and it was afterwards proved to be quite certain, that, in his infantine soul, ideas of things animate or inanimate, organic or unorganized, or of what is produced by nature or formed by art, were still strangely mingled together.

He distinguished animals from men only by their form, as men from women only by their dress; and the clothing of the female sex was, on account of its varied and striking colours, far more pleasing to him than that of males; on which account he afterwards frequently expressed his desire to become a girl; that is, to wear female apparel. That children should become grown people, was quite inconceivable to him; and he was particularly obstinate in denying this fact, when he was told that he himself had once been a little child, and that he would probably grow much taller than he then was. Nor was he convinced of its truth until some months afterwards, when repeated trials, made by marking his measure upon the wall, proved to him by experience the fact of his own, and, indeed, very rapid growth.

Not a spark of religion, not the smallest particle of any dogmatic system was to be found in his soul, how great soever the ill-timed pains might be which, immediately or in the first week after his arrival, were taken by several clergymen to seek for and to excite them. Indeed no animal could have shown itself more unable to comprehend, or to form any conception of what they meant by all their questions, discourses, and sermons, than Caspar. All the religion that he brought with him (if the name may, without scandal, be thus misapplied,) was that which the stupid piety of devout villains had furnished his pockets at his first exposure in Nuremberg.

It may, perhaps, not be uninteresting to hear the observations made on Caspar's conduct and demeanor during his abode in the tower, by a plain but sensible man, the prison-keeper Hiltel, who had the care of him for several weeks. His declaration, contained in the protocol, as far as it relates to this subject, is to the following effect: "Soon after I had for some time silently observed Caspar Hauser, as he is called, I was fully convinced that he was by no means an idiot, or one who had been neglected by nature, but that he must, in some inconceivable manner, have been deprived of all means of cultivating and developing his mind. To relate all the innumerable proofs of this which are contained in various phenomena that I have observed in Hauser's conduct, would extend my narration to too great a length. During the first days of his abode with me, his conduct was precisely that of a little child, and displayed in every respect nothing but nature and innocence. On the fourth or fifth day, he was removed from the upper and more closely confined part of the tower prison to the lower story, in which I lived with my family, and he was lodged in a small chamber which was so arranged that I could constantly observe his movements without his being able to perceive it. Here I have, in obedience to the orders given me by the burghermaster, frequently noticed his conduct when he was alone; and I have always found it to be perfectly uniform. He amused himself, when alone, with his playthings, in the same natural and unaffected manner as when he was in my presence. For, at first, when he was once fully occupied with his playthings, it was of no consequence whatever else occurred around him; for he took not the slightest notice of it. I must however remark, that the pleasure which he thus took in childish playthings, did not continue very long. When once his mind had been directed to more serious and more useful occupations, and had become accustomed to them, he no longer took delight in playing. His whole demeanour was, so to speak, a perfect mirror of childlike innocence. There was nothing deceitful in him; his expressions exactly corresponded with the dictates of his heart, that is, as far as the poverty of his language would admit of it. When once my wife and myself undressed him, in order to cleanse his body, he gave full proof of his innocence and ignorance; his conduct on that occasion was precisely that of a child; quite natural and unembarrassed.* After he had got his playthings, and other persons also had been admitted to him, I sometimes permitted my son Julius, who is eleven years old, to go to see him. He, as it were, taught him to speak, shewed him how to form his letters, and communicated to him such conceptions as he himself possessed. I also sometimes permitted my daughter Margaret, a little girl of three years old, to go into his room. He at first

* Not long afterwards, however, a feeling of modesty was awakened in him; and he then became as bashful as the most chaste and delicate maiden. An exposure of his person he now regards with horror. After the wild Brazilian girl, Isabella, whom Messrs. Spix and Martins had brought to Munich, had lived for some time among civilized people and worn clothes, it was not without much trouble, nor yet without threats and blows, that she could be brought to undress herself that her shape might be drawn by an artist.

D

took great delight in playing with her, and she taught him to string glass beads. This amusement ceased to give him satisfaction, as soon as he began to grow tired of inanimate playthings. During the latter part of his abode with me, he derived his greatest pleasure and amusement from drawings and copper-plates, which he stuck to the walls of his chamber."

CHAPTER IV.

In a very few days after his first arrival, Caspar was no longer considered in the tower as a prisoner, but as a forsaken and neglected child, who required to be cared for and educated. The prison-keeper admitted him to his family table, where, although he would not partake of any food, yet he learned to sit in a proper manner, to use his hands as a human being, and to become acquainted with, and to imitate, many of the customs of civilized life. Most willingly did he play with the children of the keeper; who, on their part, were by no means disinclined to amuse themselves with this good-natured youth, whose excessive ignorance was diverting even to children. But particularly Julius, who was eleven years old, became greatly attached to Caspar, and felt his incipient vanity not a little flattered by the occupation of teaching this robust youth—around whose chin the first rudiments of a beard had already begun to sprout—how to speak. Curiosity soon brought, every day and even every hour, multitudes of people around him, of whom few were willing to content themselves with merely gazing at the tame savage. Most of them found some means of busying themselves with him in one way or another. Some, indeed, regarded him only as an object of amusement, or of experiments by no means scientific. Yet, there were many who conversed with him rationally, and who endeavoured to awaken his mind to a communication of ideas. One pronounced words and phrases which he made him repeat, another strove by signs and gestures to make unknown things known, and unintelligible things intelligible to him. Every thing, even every plaything, by the gift of which the kind inhabitants of Nuremberg expressed their good-will and attention to the poor youth, supplied him with new materials of thought, and tended to increase the treasures of his mind, by the acquisition of new conceptions and the knowledge of significant sounds. Yet the principal advantage which accrued to him from this frequent intercourse with human beings, was its tendency to awaken his mind more and more to attention, to reflection, and to active thought, according as his self-consciousness became more clear. This, again, rendered the want of communicating his thoughts to others daily more perceptible to him; and thus, the instinctively operative and inventive teacher of languages within him, was continually kept actively employed.

About a fortnight after Caspar's arrival in Nuremberg, he was most providentially favoured with a visit from the worthy Professor Daumer, an intelligent young scholar, who, in the kindly feelings of his humane heart, discovered a peculiar vocation to devote himself to the mental development, education, and instruction of this unfortunate youth,—as far as the eager importunity of curious visitors and other impediments and interruptions permitted him to do so. Caspar would not have possessed so active a mind, so fervent a zeal to lay hold on every thing that was new to him, so vivid, so youthfully powerful, and so faithfully retentive a memory, as, to the astonishment of all, he evinced, if, with such assistance, he had not very soon learned to speak, sufficiently, at least, in some degree to express his thoughts. Yet his first attempts to speak remained for a long time a mere chopping of words, so miserably defective and so awkwardly helpless, that it was seldom possible to ascertain, with any certainty, what he meant to express by the fragments of speech which he jumbled together. Continuity of speech, or consistency of narration, was by no means to be expected from him; and much was always left to be supplied by the conjectures of the hearer. To the burghermaster, Mr. Binder, Caspar was not only an object of deep interest, in as far as his humane feelings were concerned, but he claimed his particular attention in the performance of his official duties as the head of the police; and to this most extraordinary subject of police inquiry he devoted a very large portion of his time and attention. It was indeed sufficiently apparent, that the every-day forms of official business were ill adapted to this, by no means every-day occurrence*; and that formal official inquiries and examinations could not be expected to throw any light whatsoever upon this mystery. Mr. Binder therefore very properly chose, in the present case, to avoid the embarrassing restrictions of legal forms, by means of extra-official proceedings. He caused Caspar, almost every day, to be brought to his house, and made him feel, as it were, at home in his family. He conversed with him, and made him talk as well as he could; and thus he endeavoured, by frequently questioning and cross-questioning him, to obtain some infor-

* But then the rash attempt ought not afterwards to have been made, to give, at a later period, to transactions which were only of a private nature, the apparent form of official inquiries: which gives to the public documents appertaining to this case a very singular appearance.

mation concerning the events of his life, and of his arrival. It was in this manner, that Mr. Binder at length succeeded, or thought that he had succeeded, in extracting from isolated answers and expressions of Caspar, the materials of a history, which was, on the seventh of July the same year, given to the public, in the form of an official promulgation.* This promulgation—if we may call it so—contains indeed, in many of its minute details, which have been given, and too confidently, with unnecessary prolixity, much that is incredible and contradictory. Nor is it an easy matter to discriminate, in every particular instance, between what really appertains to the person questioned, and what in fact belongs to those who questioned him;—between what really flowed from Caspar's obscure recollections, and what, by dint of repeated questions, may have been insinuated into his mind, in such a manner, as to have been involuntarily confounded by him with things actually stored up in his memory. Many incidents mentioned, may have been supplied, or may at least have received a finish, from the conjectures of others; and the introduction of many, may

* It is this promulgation, which has served for the foundation upon which all accounts that have hitherto been given of Caspar, in journals and pamphlets, have been made to rest.

even be owing to misconceptions, resulting from the impossibility of always understanding what was meant by the expressions of a half-dumb human animal, so very destitute, as Caspar was at that time, of distinct conceptions of the most common objects and every-day occurrences of nature and of life. Yet, upon the whole, that is, as far as the principal and most essential facts which it relates are concerned, this historical narrative agrees perfectly with the contents of a written memoir which was afterwards composed by Hauser himself, and sworn to by him, before a court of justice, held for the purpose of inquiring into this affair, in 1829; as it also agrees with what he has, on different occasions, invariably related to the author and to many other persons, precisely to the same effect. The account which he gave was as follows:

"He neither knows who he is nor where his home is. It was only at Nuremberg that he came into the world.* Here he first learnt that, besides himself and 'the man with whom he had always been,' there existed other men and other creatures. As long as he can recollect, he had always lived in a hole (a small low apartment, which he sometimes calls

* An expression which he often uses to designate his exposure in Nuremberg, and his first awakening to the consciousness of mental life.

a cage), where he had always sat upon the ground, with bare feet, and clothed only with a shirt and a pair of breeches.* In his apartment he never heard a sound, whether produced by a man, by an animal, or by anything else. He never saw the heavens, nor did there ever appear a brightening (daylight) such as at Nuremberg. He never perceived any difference between day and night, and much less did he ever get a sight of the beautiful lights in the heavens. Whenever he awoke from sleep, he found a loaf of bread and a pitcher of water by him. Sometimes this water had a bad taste; whenever this was the case he could no longer keep his eyes open, but was compelled to fall asleep †; and

* According to a more particular account given by Caspar —which is fully confirmed by marks upon his body which cannot be mistaken, by the singular formation of his knee and knee-hollow, and by his peculiar mode of sitting upon the ground with his legs extended, which is possible to himself alone,—he never, even in his sleep, lay with his whole body stretched out, but sat, waking and sleeping, *with his back supported in an erect posture* Some peculiar property of his place of rest, and some particular contrivance must probably have made it necessary for him to remain constantly in such a position. He is himself unable to give any further information upon this subject.

† That this water was mixed with opium may well be supposed; and the certainty that this was really the fact, was fully proved on the following occasion. After he had for some time lived with Professor Daumer, his physician

when he afterwards awoke, he found that he had a clean shirt on, and that his nails had been cut.* He never saw the face of the man who brought him his meat and drink. In his hole he had two wooden horses and several ribbons. With these horses he had always amused himself as long as he was awake; and his only occupation was, to make them run by his side, and to fix or tie the ribbons about them in different positions. Thus, one day had passed as the other; but he had never felt the want of anything, had never been sick, and — once only excepted — had never felt the⁺ sensation of pain. Upon the whole he had been much happier there than in the world, where he was obliged to suffer so much. How long he had continued to live in this situation he knew not; for he had had

attempted to administer to him a drop of opium in a glass of water. Caspar had scarcely swallowed the first mouthful of this water, when he said, " That water is nasty; it tastes exactly like the water I was sometimes obliged to drink in my cage."

* Hence, as well as from other circumstances, it is evident, that Caspar was, during his incarceration, always treated with a certain degree of careful attention. And this accounts for the attachment which he long retained to "the man with whom he had always been." This attachment ceased only at a very late period; yet never to such a degree as to make him wish that this man should be punished He wished that those should be punished by whose orders he had been confined; but he said that that man had done him no harm.

no knowledge of time. He knew not when, or how he came thither. Nor had he any recollection of ever having been in a different situation, or in any other than in that place. 'The man with whom he had always been,' never did him any harm. Yet one day, shortly before he was taken away—when he had been running his horse too hard, and had made too much noise, the man came and struck him upon his arm with a stick, or with a piece of wood; this caused the wound which he brought with him to Nuremberg.

"Pretty nearly about the same time, the man once came into his prison, placed a small table over his feet, and spread something white upon it, which he now knows to have been paper; he then came behind him, so as not to be seen by him, took hold of his hand, and moved it backwards and forwards on the paper, with a thing (a lead pencil) which he had stuck between his fingers. He (Hauser) was then ignorant of what it was; but he was mightily pleased when he saw the black figures which began to appear upon the white paper. When he felt that his hand was free, and the man was gone from him, he was so much pleased with his new discovery, that he could never grow tired of drawing these figures repeatedly upon the paper. This occupation made him almost neglect his horses, although he did not know what those characters signified. The man repeated his visits in the same manner several times.*

" Another time the man came again, lifted him from the place where he lay, placed him on his feet, and endeavoured to teach him to

* Of the fact that Caspar really had had instruction, and, indeed, regular elementary instruction in writing, he gave evident proofs immediately on the first morning after his arrival in Nuremberg. When the prison-keeper, Hiltel, came to him that morning in the prison, he gave him, in order to employ or to amuse him, a sheet of paper with a lead pencil. Caspar seized eagerly on both, placed the paper upon the bench, and began and continued to write, without intermission, and without ever looking up, or suffering himsslf to be disturbed by anything that passed, until he had filled the whole folio sheet, on all four sides, with his writing. The appearance of this sheet, which has been preserved and affixed to the documents furnished by the police, is much the same as if Caspar, who nevertheless wrote from memory, had had a copy lying before him, such as are commonly set before children when they are first taught to write. For the writing upon this sheet consisted of rows of letters, or rows of syllables, so that almost everywhere, the same letter or the same syllable is constantly repeated. At the bottom of each page, all the letters of the alphabet are also placed together, in the same order in which they actually succeed each other, as is commonly the case in copies given to children: and, in another line, the numerical cyphers are placed, from 1 to 0, in their proper order On one page of this sheet the name " Kaspar Hauser " is constantly repeated ; and, on the same sheet, the word reider (Renter, rider) frequently occurs, yet this sheet also proves that Caspar had not advanced beyond the first elements of writing.

stand. This he repeated at several different times. The manner in which he effected this was the following : he seized him firmly around the breast from behind; placed his feet behind Caspar's feet, and lifted them, as in stepping forward.

"Finally, the man appeared once again, placed Caspar's hands over his shoulders, tied them fast, and thus carried him on his back out of the prison. He was carried up (or down) a hill.* He knows not how he felt; all became night, and he was laid upon his back." This " becoming night," as appeared on many different occasions at Nuremberg, signified, in Caspar's language, " to faint away." The account given of the continuation of his journey, is principally confined to the following particulars : " that he had often lain with his face to the ground, in which cases it became night; that he had several times eaten bread and drunk water; that 'the

---

* It is evident, and other circumstances prove it to be a fact, that Caspar could not at that time yet distinguish the motion of ascending from that of descending, or height from depth, even as to the impressions made upon his own feelings; and that he was consequently still less able to designate this difference correctly by means of words. What Caspar calls a hill, must, in all probability, have been a flight of stairs. Caspar also thinks he can recollect that, in being carried, he brushed against something by his side.

man with whom he had always been,' had often taken pains to teach him to walk, which always gave him great pain," &c. This man never spoke to him, excepting that he continually repeated to him the words, " Reuta wähn," &c.* He (Caspar) never saw the face of the man either on this journey or ever before in prison. Whenever he led him he directed him to look down upon the ground and at his feet,—an injunction which he always strictly obeyed, partly from fear, and partly because his attention was sufficiently occupied with his own person and the position of his feet. Not long before he was observed at Nuremberg, the man had put the clothes upon him which he then wore.

The putting on of his boots gave him great pain; for the man made him sit on the ground, seized him from behind, drew his feet up, and thus forced them into the boots. They then proceeded onwards still more miserably than before. He neither then, nor ever before, perceived any thing of the objects around him; he neither observed nor saw them; and therefore he could not tell from what part of the country, in what direction, or by which way he came. All that he was conscious of

---

* This jargon seems to imply, " I will be a rider (a trooper) as my father was."

was, that the man who had been leading him put the letter which he had brought with him into his hand, and then vanished; after which a citizen observed him and took him to the guard-room at the New-gate. This history of the mysterious imprisonment and exposure of a young man, presents, not only a fearful, but a most singular and obscure enigma, which may indeed give rise to innumerable questions and conjectures, but, in respect to which, little can be said with certainty; and which, until its solution shall have been found, must continue to retain, in common with all enigmas, the property of being enigmatical. Caspar's mental condition, during his dungeon-life, must have been that of a human being immersed in his infancy, in a profound sleep, in which he was not conscious even of a dream, or at least of any succession of dreams. He had continued in this stupor until, affrighted with pain and apprehensions, he suddenly awoke, stunned with the wild and confused noises and the unintelligible impressions of a variegated world, without knowing what had happened. Whoever should expect that such a being, when arrived at a full state of consciousness, should be able to give a perfectly clear and circumstantial historical description of his slumbers and his dreams, which should satisfy the understanding, so as to remove every doubt, would expect nothing less than that a sleeper should, sleeping, have been awake, or that a waking person should, while awake, have slept.

There are still certain regions in Germany, to which, if a second Dupin were to furnish maps depicting the illumination of the human mind in different countries, he would give a colouring of dark gray, where occurrences similar to those which Hauser has related, are by no means unheard of. Dr. Horn*, for instance, saw in the infirmary at Salzburg, but a few years ago, a girl of twenty-two years of age, and by no means ugly, who had been brought up in a hog-stye among the hogs, and who had sat there for many years with her legs crossed. One of her legs was quite crooked, she grunted like a hog, and her gestures were brutishly unseemly in a human dress. In comparison with such abominations, the crimes committed against Caspar Hauser may even be considered as acts in which the forbearance of humanity is still visible. That Caspar should be unable to give any account of the mode and manner in which he was conveyed to Nuremberg, or to furnish any recitals or descriptions of the adventures of his jour-

* In his travels through Germany. (See Gottingsche gelehrte Anzeige. July, 1831. p. 1097.)

ney, of the places through which he passed, or of any of the usual occurrences which strike the attention of travellers, whatever may be their mode of conveyance, is so far from being astonishing, that the case could not have been otherwise without the intervention of a miracle. Even if Caspar had, before he left his prison, awoke to a state of clear and rational self-consciousness; if, like Sigismund in his tower, he had, by means of education and the cultivation of his mind, attained to the maturity of a young man, yet the sudden transition from the close confinement and gloomy obscurity of his dungeon, could not have failed to have thrown him either into fainting fits or into a state very similar to that of excessive intoxication. The unwonted impressions made by the external air must have stunned him, and the bright sun-light blinded his eyes. Yet even with seeing and unblinded eyes, he would have seen nothing; at least he would have observed and taken cognizance of nothing. For nature, with all her phenomena, must at that time have shone before his eyes, with the glare of one confusedly diversified and checkered mass, in which no single object could be distinguished from another. That this was really the case, even at Nuremberg, was, as we shall see hereafter, confirmed in the most unequivocal manner by actual experience. From what part of the country was Caspar brought? upon what road and through which gate did he arrive? was his journey performed on foot, or in a carriage or a waggon? To these and to similar questions, the answers, even if they could be given with perfect certainty, would be such as would interest rather the judge who might be called upon to examine and to decide, than the public. Caspar himself remembers only his having walked; without, however, being able to add anything which might lead to probable conjectures concerning the time consumed, or the length of the way passed over in walking. That he has no recollection of having rode in a carriage or waggon, does not, however, prove that he may not, nevertheless, and perhaps for the greater part of the way, have been thus conveyed. Caspar sinks, even yet, whenever he rides in a carriage or a waggon, into a kind of death sleep, from which he does not easily awake, whether the vehicle stops or rolls on; and, in this state, how roughly soever it may be done, he may be lifted up or laid down, and packed or unpacked, without his having the least perception of it. When sleep has once laid hold of him, no noise, no sound, no report, no thunder, is loud enough to wake him. If

Caspar, which, from his own account, appears probable, fainted away whenever he was brought into the open air; if his conductors, for the sake of greater security, had made him drink some of the ill-tasted water (opium diluted with water), they may, with the greatest safety, have thrown him into a waggon and driven him many a day's journey, without any fear of his awakening, crying out, or occasioning his kidnappers the least inconvenience. M. Schmidt von Lubeck, has, in his book Uber Kaspar Hauser* (Altona, 1831), given many ingenious reasons for supposing that Caspar was brought to Nuremberg from some place in its immediate vicinity. For this, as well as for other conjectures, this history leaves ample room. That the person by whom Caspar was brought to Nuremberg, must have been one who was well acquainted with the city and its locality, is certain; and that he must in former times have served as a soldier in one of the regiments stationed there, is at least highly probable.

The crimes committed against Caspar Hauser, as far as the information hitherto given of them extends, are, judging according to the criminal code of Bavaria, the following:

* Many curious conjectures as to the place of Hauser's confinement, &c. &c., taken from the work here mentioned, will be found in the Appendix.

I. *The crime of illegal imprisonment:* (Strafgesetzbuch Thl. 1 Art. 192—695) which was doubly aggravated, first, in respect to the *duration* of the imprisonment, which appears to have lasted from his earliest infancy to the age of early manhood; and, secondly, in respect to its *kind,* inasmuch as it was connected with particular instances of *ill-treatment.* As such, we must consider, not only the brutish den and crippling position to which he was confined, and his coarse diet, which would scarcely have satisfied a dog, but we must incontestably, and indeed principally, regard as such, the cruel withholding from him of the most ordinary gifts, which nature wtih a liberal hand, extends even to the most indigent;—the depriving him of all the means of mental development and culture,—the unnatural detention of a human soul in a state of irrational animality. With this crime concurs, objectively—

II. The crime of *exposure:* which, according to Stgb. Thl. 1 Art. 174, may be committed not only in regard to infants, but also in regard to grown up persons, whom sickness or other infirmities render unable to help themselves; among which class of persons, Caspar, on account of the state of animal stupidity and of inability to see with his eyes open, or even to walk in an upright position with safety, in which he then was, must undoubtedly be reckoned. The crime of Caspar's exposure is also aggravated by the consideration of the danger to which it subjected his life. His situation, both in respect to his mind and his body, rendered him evidently liable to the danger, either of falling into the river Pzegnitz, which was very near to the place of his exposure, or of being run down by carriages or horses. If a particular crime, affecting the mental powers, or, as it might more properly be designated, affecting the life of a human soul, were known to the criminal code of Bavaria; this crime would, in forming a juridical estimate of this case, when compared with the crime of illegal imprisonment, assume the place of the highest importance; nay, the latter crime would vanish in comparison with the first, as infinitely the greater of the two, and it would be absorbed by it.* The depriva-

* The conception that a crime may be absorbed by the commission of a greater crime, is familiar to German writers on criminal jurisprudence. If a person found guilty of petty larceny, were also found guilty of murder, it is evident that the punishment of death incurred by the second crime, would render it impossible to inflict the punishment of imprisonment incurred by the first; which, by suspending his execution, would act rather as a reprieve than as a punishment. The first crime would therefore remain unpunished; its punishment being, as it were, absorbed by the punishment of the second crime.

tion of external liberty, though in itself an irreparable injury, yet bears no comparison with the injury done to this unhappy being, by depriving him of the incalculable sum of inestimable benefits which can never be restored to him, and which, by the robbery committed upon his freedom, and the mode and manner in which it was done, were either entirely withdrawn from him, or destroyed, and his means of enjoying them miserably crippled for the remainder of his life. Such a crime does not merely affect the external corporeal appearance of man, but the inmost essence of his spiritual being; it is the iniquity of a murderous robbery perpetrated upon the very sanctuary of his rational nature. When some authors designate such a crime merely by the predicate of a robbery of the intellect (noochiria), as Titmann*, and make that which constitutes the essential condition of its existence, to consist in actually effecting a deprivation of intellect, or in causing insanity; Caspar Hauser's case furnishes an instance which may convince them, that their conception of this crime is far too limited, and that a legislator, who should desire to render his system more complete, by the exhibition of such a genus of crimes, ought to assume a more elevated and more extensive point of

* Handbuch der Strafrechtswissenschaft, Thl. 1, § 179.

view. The confinement which Caspar suffered in his infancy, produced neither idiotcy nor insanity; for, since the recovery of his liberty, as we shall see more particular hereafter, he has emerged from the mere animal state; his mind has been developed, and he may now, with certain limitations, be considered as a rational, intelligent, civilized, and moral man. Yet no one can help perceiving, that it is the criminal invasion of the life of his soul,— that it is the iniquity perpetrated against the higher principles of his spiritual nature, which presents the most revolting aspect of the crime committed against him. An attempt, by artificial contrivances, to exclude a man from nature and from all intercourse with rational beings, to change the course of his human destiny, and to withdraw from him all the nourishment afforded by those spiritual substances which nature has appointed for food to the human mind, that it may grow and flourish, and be instructed, and developed, and formed;—such an attempt must, considered even quite independently of its actual consequences, be, in itself, a highly criminal invasion of man's most sacred and most peculiar property,— the freedom and the destiny of his soul. But, above all, the following consideration must be added to the rest. Caspar, having been sunk during the whole of the earlier part of his life in animal sleep, has passed through this extensive and beautiful part of it, without having lived through it. His existence was, during all this time, similar to that of a person really dead; in having slept through his youthful years, they have passed by him, without his having had them in his possession; because he was rendered unable to become conscious of their existence. This chasm, which crime has torn in his life, cannot any more be filled up; that time, in which he omitted to live, can never be brought back, that it may yet be lived through; that juvenility, which fled while his soul was asleep, can never be overtaken. How long soever he may live, he must for ever remain a man without childhood and boyhood; a monstrous being, who, contrary to the usual course of nature, only began to live in the middle of his life. Inasmuch as all the earlier part of his life was thus taken from him, he may be said to have been the subject of a partial soul-murder. The deed done to Caspar differs from the crime that would be committed by one who should plunge a man of sound intellect, at a later period, into a state of stupid idiotcy, unconsciousness, or irrationality, only in respect to the different epoch of life at which the blow of soul-murder was struck; in one instance, the life of a human soul was mutilated at its commeucement; in the other it would be mutilated at its close. Besides, one of the chief momenta, which ought not to be overlooked, is this: since childhood and boyhood are given and destined by nature for the development and perfection of our mental as well as our corporeal life, and since nature overleaps nothing, the consequence of Caspar's having come into the world as a child, at the age of early manhood, is, that the different states of life which in other men are formed and developed gradually, have in him, both now and for ever been, as it were, displaced and improperly joined together. Having commenced the life of infancy at the age of physical maturity, he will, throughout all his life, remain, as regards his mind, less forward than his age, and, as regards his age, more forward than his mind. Mental and physical life, which, in the regular course of their natural development, go hand in hand, have, therefore, in respect to Caspar, been, as it were, separated, and placed in unnatural opposition to each other. Because he *slept* through his childhood, that childhood could not be *lived* through by him at its proper time; it therefore still remains to be lived through by him; and it consequently follows him into his later years, not as a smiling genius, but as a terrifying spectre, which is constantly intruding upon him at an unseasonable hour. If, besides all this, we take into consideration the devastation which the fate of his earlier youth, as will more fully be seen hereafter, has occasioned in his mind, it must appear evident, from the instance here given, that the conception of a robbery committed upon the intellect, does by no means exhaust the conception of a crime committed against the life of the soul.

What other crimes may, perhaps, yet lie concealed behind the iniquity committed against Caspar? What were the ends which Hauser's secret imprisonment was intended to subserve?—To answer these questions, would lead us too far either into the airy regions of conjecture, or within certain confines which will not admit of such an exposure to the light.

This crime, which, in the history of human atrocities is still almost unheard of, presents to the learned judge, as well as to the juridical physician, yet another very remarkable aspect. Scrutinies and judgments concerning certain states of mind, regard commonly only the criminal himself; inasmuch as their only end is to ascertain whether his actions are imputable to him or not. But here an instance is given of a most extraordinary, and, in its kind, exclusively singular case, in which the matter of fact that is to prove the existence of a crime, lies almost entirely concealed within a human soul; where it can be investigated and established only by means of inquiries purely psychological, and founded upon observations indicating certain states of the thinking and sentient mind of the person injured. Even of the history of this deed, we have as yet no other knowledge, than that which we have received from the narration given of it by him to whom it was done: yet the truth of this narration is warranted by the personality of the narrator himself; upon whose thinking and sentient mind (geist und gemüth)—as we shall see more particularly hereafter—the deed itself, is written in visible and legible characters. No other being than one who has experienced and suffered what Caspar has, can be what Caspar is; and he whose being indicates what Caspar does, must have lived in a state such as that in which Caspar says that he lived. And thus we see an instance in which our estimation of the degree of credit which we are to give to the narrator of an almost incredible occurrence, is made to rest almost altogether upon psychological grounds. But the evidence furnished in this instance upon such grounds, outweighs that of any other proof. Witnesses may lie, documents may be falsified; but no other human being, except indeed he were a magician armed with a certain portion of omnipotence and omniscience, is able to produce a lie of such a nature, that, in whatever aspect you may present it to the light, it shall appear, in all of them, as the purest and most uncontaminated truth, as the very personification of truth itself. Whoever should doubt Caspar's narration, must doubt Caspar's person. But, such a sceptic might with equal reason be permitted to doubt whether a person, bleeding from a hundred wounds, and convulsed before his eyes with the agonies of death, was really a wounded and dying man, or was only acting the part of a wounded and dying man. Yet we must not anticipate the reader's judgment; my exhibition of Caspar's person has only just commenced.

CHAPTER V.

Caspar had been already considerably more than a month at Nuremberg, when, among the latest novelties of the day, I heard of this foundling. No official accounts of this occurrence had yet been received by the highest authorities of the province; it was therefore only as a private individual, and from a general regard to the interests of humanity and of science, that I went to Nuremberg on the 11th of July, 1828, in order to examine this most extraordinary and singular phenomenon. Caspar's abode was at that time still in the Lugisland at the Vestner-gate, where every body was admitted who desired to see him. In fact, from morning to night, Caspar attracted scarcely fewer visitors than the kangaroo, or the tame hyena, in the celebrated menagerie of M. von Aken. I therefore also proceeded thither, in company with Col. von D——, two ladies, and two children; and we fortunately arrived there at an hour when no other visitors happened to be present. Caspar's abode was in a small but cleanly and light room, the windows of which opened upon an extensive and pleasant prospect. We found him with his feet bare, clothed, besides his shirt, only with a pair of old trousers. The walls of his chamber had been decorated by Caspar, as high as he could reach, with sheets of coloured pictures. He stuck them to the wall, every morning anew, with his saliva, which was, at that time, as tough as glue*; and, as soon as it became twilight, he took them down again, and laid them together by his side. In a corner of the fixed bench, which extended around the room, was his bed, which consisted of a bag of straw, with a pillow and blanket. The whole of the remaining part of the bench was thickly covered with a variety of playthings, with hundreds of leaden soldiers, wooden dogs, horses, and other toys, such as are commonly manufactured at Nuremberg. They had already ceased to occupy much of his attention during the day; yet he was at no little trouble to gather carefully together all these trifles, and all their trifling appurtenances, every evening; to unpack them, as soon as he awoke, and to place them in a certain order, in rows alongside of each other. The benevolent feelings

---

* The saliva was so very gluey that in taking these sheets down, parts of them sometimes adhered to the wall and sometimes parts of the plastering of the wall adhered to the paper.

of the kind inhabitants of Nuremberg had also induced them to present him with various articles of wearing apparel, which he kept under his pillow, and displayed to us with a childish pleasure not unmingled with some little vanity. Upon the bench there lay, mingled with these playthings, several pieces of money, to which, however, he paid no attention. From these I took a soiled crown piece, and a quite new piece of twenty-four kreutzers* in my hand, and asked him which of these he liked best? He chose the small shining one; he said the larger one was ugly, and he regarded it with a look expressive of aversion. When I endeavoured to make him understand that the larger piece was, nevertheless, the more valuable of the two, and that he could get more pretty things for it than for the smaller one, he listened indeed attentively, and assumed, for some time, a thoughtful stare; but at length he told me, that he did not know what I meant.

When we entered into his apartment, he showed nothing like shyness or timidity; on the contrary, he met us with confidence, and seemed to be rejoiced at our visit. He

* A crown piece is about the size of a Spanish dollar, and a piece of twenty-four kreutzers, about the size of a quarter of a dollar.

first of all noticed the Colonel's bright uniform, and he could not cease to admire his helmet, which glittered with gold; then the coloured dresses of the ladies attracted his attention; as for myself, being dressed in a modest black frock coat, I was at first scarcely honoured with a single glance. Each of us placed himself separately before him, and mentioned to him his name and title. Whenever any person was thus introduced, Caspar went up very close to him, regarded him with a sharp staring look, noticed every particular part of his face, as his forehead, eyes, nose, mouth, chin, &c., successively, with a penetrating rapid glance, and, as I could distinctly perceive, at the very last, he collected all the different parts of the countenance, which at first he had gathered separately and piece by piece, into one whole. He then repeated the name of the person as it had been mentioned to him. And now he knew the person; and, as experience afterwards proved, he knew him for ever. He averted his eyes, as much as possible, from every glare of light, and he most carefully avoided the rays of the sun which entered directly through the window. When such a ray accidentally struck his eye, he winked very much, wrinkled his forehead, and evidently showed that he was in pain.

His eyes were also much inflamed, and he betrayed in every respect the greatest sensibility of the effects of light.

Although his face became afterwards perfectly regular, yet at that time a striking difference was perceptible between the left and the right side of it. The first was perceptibly drawn awry and distorted, and convulsive spasms frequently passed over it like flashes of lightning. By these spasms the whole left side of his body, and particularly his arm and hand were visibly affected.

If anything was shown to him which excited his curiosity, if any word was spoken which struck his attention, or was unintelligible to him, these spasms immediately made their appearance, and they were generally succeeded by a kind of nervous rigidity. He then stood motionless; not a muscle of his face moved; his eyes remained wide open without winking, and assumed a lifeless stare; he appeared, like a statue, to be unable to see, to hear, or to be excited to any living movement by external impressions. This state was observable whenever he was meditating upon any thing, whenever he was seeking the idea corresponding to any new word, or the word corresponding to any new thing; or whenever he endeavoured to connect any thing that was unknown to him with something that he knew, in order to render the first conceivable by the means of the latter.

His enunciation of words which he knew, was plain and determinate, without hesitating or stammering. But coherent speech was not yet to be expected from him, and his language was as indigent as his stock of ideas. It was therefore also extremely difficult to become intelligible to him. Scarcely had any one uttered a few sentences which he appeared to understand, when it was found that something was mingled with them which was foreign to him, and if he wished to understand it, his spasms immediately returned. In all that he said, the conjunctions, participles, and adverbs, were still almost entirely wanting; his conjugation embraced little more than the infinitive; and he was most of all deficient in respect to his syntax, which was in a state of miserable confusion. " Caspar very well," instead of, I am very well; " Caspar shall Julie tell," instead of, I will tell it to Julius (the son of the prison-keeper); such were his common modes of expressing himself. The pronoun I occurred very rarely; he generally spoke of himself in the third person, calling himself Caspar. In the same manner, he also spoke to others in the third person instead of the second; for instance, in speaking to a colonel or a lady, instead of saying you, he would say colonel or lady such a one, using the verb in the third person. Thus also, in speaking to him, if you wished him immediately to understand whom you meant, you must not say *you* to him, but Caspar. The same word was often used by him in different significations, which occasioned ludicrous mistakes. Many words which signify only a particular species, would be applied by him to the whole genus. Thus, for instance, he would use the word hill or mountain, as if it applied to every protuberance or elevation; and in consequence thereof, he once called a corpulent gentleman, whose name he could not recollect, "the man with the great mountain." A lady, the end of whose shawl he once saw dragging on the floor, he called "the lady with the beautiful tail."

It may be supposed, that I did not omit, by various questions, to obtain from him some account of his past life. But all that I could draw from him was so confused and so undeterminate a jargon, that, being yet unaccustomed to his manner of speaking, I could mostly only guess what he meant, while much remained that was utterly unintelligible to me.

It appeared to me not unimportant to make

some trial of his taste in respect to different colours; he shewed that in this particular also, he was of the same mind as children and those who are called savages. The red colour, and indeed the most glaring red, was preferred by him to every other; the yellow he disliked, excepting when it struck the sight as shining gold, in which case his choice wavered between this colour and the glaring red; white was indifferent to him, but green appeared to him almost as detestable as black. This taste, and particularly his predilection for the red colour, he retained, as Professor Daumer's later observations prove, long after the cultivation of his mind had very considerably advanced. If the choice had been given him, he would have clothed himself, and all for whom he had a regard, from head to foot in scarlet or purple. The appearance of nature, green being the principal colour of her garment, gave him no delight. She could appear beautiful to him only when viewed through a red-coloured glass. With Professor Daumer's dwelling, to which shortly after my visit he was removed from the Lug-island, he was not much pleased; because the only prospect that he had there was the garden, where he saw nothing but ugly trees and plants, as he called them. On the contrary, he was particularly pleased with the dwelling of one of his preceptor's friends, which was situated in a narrow unpleasant street, because opposite to, and round about it, nothing was to be seen but houses beautifully painted red. When a tree full of red apples was shewn him, he expressed much satisfaction at seeing it; yet he thought that it would have been still more beautiful if its leaves also were as red as the fruit. Seeing a person once drinking red wine, he expressed a wish that he, who drank nothing but water, could also drink things which appeared so beautiful.

There was but one advantage more which he wished that his favourite animals, horses, possessed:—it was, that instead of being black, bay, or white, their colour was scarlet. The curiosity, the thirst for knowledge, and the inflexible perseverance with which he fixed his attention to any thing that he was determined to learn or comprehend, surpassed every thing that can be conceived of them; and the manner in which they were expressed was truly affecting. It has already been stated, that he no longer employed himself in the day-time with his playthings; his hours throughout the day were successively occupied with writing, with drawing, or with other instructive employments in which Professor Daumer engaged him. Bitterly did he complain to us, that the great number of people who visited him left him no time to learn any thing. It was very affecting to hear his often-repeated lamentation, that the people in the world knew so much, and that there were so very many things which he had not yet learnt. Next to writing, drawing was his favourite occupation, for which he evinced a great capacity joined with equal perseverance. For several days past he had undertaken the task of copying a lithographic print of the burghermaster Binder. A large packet of quarter sheets had already been filled with the copies which he had drawn; they were arranged in a long series, in the order in which they had been produced. I examined each of them separately; the first attempts resembled exactly the pictures drawn by little children, who imagine that they have drawn a face when they have scratched upon the paper something meant to represent an oval figure, with a few long and cross strokes. Yet in almost every one of the succeeding attempts, some improvments were distinctly visible; so that these lines began more and more to resemble a human countenance, and finally represented the original, though still in a crude and imperfect manner, yet so that their resemblance to it might be recognised. I expressed my approbation of some of his last attempts; but he shewed that he was not satisfied, and insinuated that he should be obliged to draw the picture a great many times before it would be drawn as it ought to be, and then he would make it a present to the burghermaster.

With his life in the world he appeared to be by no means satisfied; he longed to go back to " the man with whom he had always been." At home (in his hole), he said, he had never suffered so much from head-ache, and had never been so much teazed as since he was in the world. By this, he alluded to the unpleasant and painful sensations which were occasioned by the many new impressions to which he was totally unaccustomed, and by a great variety of smells which were disagreeable to him, &c.; as well as to the numerous visits of those who came to see him from curiosity, to their incessant questioning of him, and to some of their inconsiderate and not very humane experiments. He had therefore no fault to find with " the man with whom he had always been," except that he had not yet come to take him back again, and that he had never shewn him or told him any thing of so many beautiful things which there are in the world. He is willing to remain in Nuremberg, until he has learnt what the burghermaster and the professor (Daumer) know; but then the burghermaster must take him home, and then he will shew the man what he has learnt in the meantime. When I expressed my surprise that he should wish to return to that abominably bad man, he replied with mild indignation, " Man not bad, man me no bad done."

Of his astonishing memory, which is as quick as it is tenacious, he gave us the most striking proofs. In noticing any of the numerous things, whether small or great, which were in his possession, he was able to mention the name and the title of the person who had given it to him; and if several persons were to be mentioned, whose surnames were alike, he distinguished them accurately, by their Christian names, or by other marks of distinction. About an hour after we had seen him, we met him again in the street, it being about the time when he was conducted to the burghermaster's. We addressed him; and when we asked him whether he could recollect our names? he mentioned, without the least hesitation, the full name of every one of the company, together with all our titles, which must, nevertheless, have appeared to him as unintelligible nonsense. His physician, Dr. Osterhausen, observed, on a different occasion, that when a nosegay had been given him, and he had been told the names of all the different flowers of which it was composed, he recognised, several days afterwards, every one of these flowers, and he was able to tell the name of each of them. But the strength of his memory decreased afterwards, precisely in proportion as it was enriched, and as the labour of his understanding was increased. His obedience to all those persons who had acquired paternal authority over him, particularly to the burghermaster, Professor Daumer, and the prison-keeper, Hiltel, was unconditional and boundless. That the burghermaster, or the professor, had said so, was to him a reason for doing or omitting to do anything, which was final and totally exclusive of all farther questions and considerations. When once I asked him, Why he thought himself obliged always to yield such punctual obedience? he replied, " The man with whom I always was, taught me that I must do as I am bidden." Yet, in his opinion, this submission to the authority of others, referred only to what he was to do or not to do, and it had no connexion whatever with his knowing, believing, and judging. Before he could acknowledge any thing to be certain and true, it was necessary that he should be convinced; and, indeed, that he should be convinced, either by the intuition of his senses, or by some reasoning adapted to his powers of comprehension, and to the scanty acquirements of his almost vacant mind, as to appear to him to be striking. Whenever it was impossible to reach his understanding by any of these ways, he did not, indeed, contradict the assertion made, but he would leave the matter undecided, until, as he used to say, he had learned more. I spoke to him, among other things, of the impending winter, and I told him that the roofs of the houses, and the streets of the city, would then be all white—as white as the walls of his chamber. He said that this would be very pretty; but he plainly insinuated that he should not believe it before he had seen it. The next winter, when the first snow fell, he expressed great joy, that the streets, the roofs, and the trees, had now been so well painted; and he went quickly down into the yard, to fetch some of the white paint; but he soon ran to his preceptor, with all his fingers stretched out, crying, and blubbering, and bawling out, " that the white paint had bit his hand."

A most surprising and inexplicable property

of this young man, was his love of order and cleanliness, which he even carried to the extreme of pedantry. Of the many hundreds of trifles of which his little household consisted, each had its appropriate place, was properly packed, carefully folded, symmetrically arranged, &c. Uncleanliness, or whatever he considered as such, whether in his own person or in others, was an abomination to him. He observed almost every grain of dust upon our clothes; and when he once saw a few grains of snuff on my frill, he shewed them to me, briskly indicating that he wished me to wipe those nasty things away.

The most remarkable fact of experience in respect to him which I learnt, but which was not fully explained to me until several years afterwards, was the result of the following experiment, which was suggested to me by a very obvious association of ideas, leading me to compare what was observable in Caspar, who had not come forth from his dark dungeon to the light of day before the age of early manhood, with the well-known account, given by Cheselden, of a young man who had become blind but a few days after his birth, and who, in consequence of a successful operation, had been restored to sight nearly at the same age.

I directed Caspar to look out of the window,

pointing to the wide and extensive prospect of a beautiful landscape that presented itself to us in all the glory of summer; and I asked him whether what he saw was not very beautiful. He obeyed; but he instantly drew back, with visible horror, exclaiming, "Ugly! ugly!" and then pointing to the white wall of his chamber, he said, "There are not ugly." To my question, Why it was ugly? no other reply was made, but, "Ugly! ugly!" and thus nothing remained, for the present, for me to do, but to take care to preserve this circumstance in my memory, and to expect its explanation at the time when Caspar should be better able to express what he meant to say. That his turning away from the prospect pointed at could not be sufficiently accounted for, by the painful impression made upon his optic nerve by the light, appeared to me to be evident; for his countenance at this time did not so much express pain as horror and dismay. Besides, he stood at some distance from the window, by the side of it, so that although he could see the prospect pointed at, yet, in looking at it, he could not be exposed to the impression made by rays of light entering directly into the window. When Caspar, afterwards, in 1831, spent some weeks with me, at my own house, where I had continual opportunities of observing him accurately, and of completing and correcting the results of former observations, I took an opportunity of conversing with him respecting this occurrence. I asked him whether he remembered my visit to him at the tower; and whether he could particularly recollect the circumstance, that I had asked him how he liked the prospect from his window, and that he had turned from it with horror, and had repeatedly exclaimed, "Ugly! ugly!" and I then asked him, Why he had done so ? and what had then appeared to him? To which he replied, " Yes, indeed, what I then saw was very ugly. For when I looked at the window, it always appeared to me as if a window-shutter had been placed close before my eyes, upon which a wall-painter had spattered the contents of his different brushes, filled with white, blue, green, yellow, and red paint, all mingled together. Single things, as I now see things, I could not at that time recognise and distinguish from each other. This was shocking to look at; and besides, it made me feel anxious and uneasy; because it appeared to me as if my window had been closed up with this party-coloured shutter, in order to prevent me from looking out into the open air. That what I then saw were fields, hills, and houses; that many things which at that time appeared to me much larger, were, in fact, much smaller, while many other things that appeared smaller, were, in reality, larger than other things, is a fact of which I was afterwards convinced by the experience gained during my walks; at length I no longer saw anything more of the shutter."

To other questions he replied, that in the beginning he could not distinguish between what was really round or triangular, and what was only painted as round or triangular. The men and horses represented on sheets of pictures, appeared to him precisely as the men and horses that were carved in wood; the first as round as the latter, or these as flat as those. But he said, that, in the packing and unpacking of his things, he had soon felt a difference; and that afterwards, it had seldom happened to him to mistake the one for the other.

Here, then, we behold, in Caspar, a living instance of Cheselden's blind man who had recovered his sight. Let us hear what Voltaire*, or Diderot†, who, in this instance, may pass

In his Philosophie de Newton (Oeuvres complètes Gotha, 1786, T. xxxi. p. 118, &c.)

† Lettres sur les aveugles à l'usage de ceux qui voyent (Londres, 149) p. 1759—64. Diderot has copied Voltaire's account verbatim.

for the same person as Voltaire, has said of this blind person.* "The young man whose cataracts were couched by this skilful surgeon, did not for a long time distinguish either magnitudes, distances, or even figures from each other. An object of an inch in size, which, when placed before his eyes, concealed a house from his view, appeared to him as large as that house. All objects were present to his eye, and appeared to him to be applied to that organ, as objects of touch are applied to the skin. He could not distinguish, by his sight, what, by the aid of his hands, he had judged to be round, from what he had judged to be angular; nor could he, by means of his eyes, discern whether what, by his feelings, he had perceived to be above or below, was, in fact, above or below. He attained, though not without some difficulty, to a perception, that his house was larger than his chamber; but he could never conceive, how the eye could give him this information. Many repeated facts of experience were required, in order to satisfy him that paintings represented solid bodies; and when, by dint of looking at pictures, he was convinced that what he saw before him were merely surfaces, he felt them with his

* The author was unable to obtain Cheselden's original work.

hands, and was then much surprised to find only a plain surface without any projection. He then would ask which of his senses deceived him, his touch or his sight? Painting has, however, sometimes produced the same effect upon savages the first time that they saw it: they took painted figures for living men, interrogated them, and were quite astonished to find that they received no answer; an error which in them certainly could not have proceeded from their being unaccustomed to the sight of visible objects."

To little children, also, during the first weeks or months after their birth, every thing appears equally near. They will extend their little hands to reach the glittering ball of a distant steeple, and they know neither how to distinguish things that are actually great or small, from things that are apparently so, nor how to distinguish real from painted objects. For, in respect to objects both of the sight and of the touch, it is necessary that both of these senses should mutually assist each other, in order to enable us to recognise them for what they really are. The explanation of this fact of experience depends upon the elementary law of all vision, regarding which the great English philosopher, Berkley, has expressed himself in the following manner: " It is, I think, agreed by all, that distance, of itself, and immediately, cannot be seen. For distance being a line directed end-wise to the eye, it projects only one point at the bottom of the eye. Which point remains invariably the same, whether the distance be longer or shorter. I find it also acknowledged, that the estimate we make of the distance of objects considerably remote, is rather an act of judgment grounded on experience, than of sense. For example: when I perceive a great number of intermediate objects, such as houses, fields, rivers, and the like, which I have experienced to take up a considerable space; I thence form a judgment or conclusion, that the object I see beyond them is at a great distance. Again, when an object appears faint and small, which, at a near distance, I have experienced to make a vigorous and large appearance, I instantly conclude it to be far off. And this, it is evident, is the result of experience; without which, from the faintness and littleness, I should not have inferred any thing concerning the distance of objects." The application of this law of optics, and of those facts, in explaining the delusion of the senses which Caspar experienced, is obvious. As Caspar had never before been accustomed to walk further than from the tower to the burghermaster's house, or, perhaps, through one or two streets more; as, in consequence of the irritability of his eyes, and of his fear of falling, he always looked down at his feet, and as, on account of his sensibility of the light, he always avoided looking out into the vast ocean of light around him, he had, for a length of time, no opportunity of gaining experience concerning the perspective and the distances of visible objects. All the numerous things in the country at which he was looking, which, together with a comparatively small portion of the blue sky, filled the aperture between the upper and lower window frame, must, therefore, have presented themselves to him as a great variety of formless and equally distant phenomena, arranged the one above the other. Hence the whole must have been viewed by him as an upright table, upon which numerous and differently coloured objects of different sizes, had assumed the appearance of shapeless and party-coloured blots.

CHAPTER VI.

Though Caspar Hauser's almost constant and uninterrupted intercourse with the numerous individuals who thronged to him at all hours of the day, was unquestionably attended with the advantage of making him acquainted, in a short and easy manner, with a great variety of things and words, and of thus enabling him to make very rapid progress in learning how to speak with others, and to understand them; yet it is equally certain, that the heterogeneous influence of mingled masses of individuals to which he was thus constantly exposed, was by no means well adapted to promote an orderly development of this neglected youth, in agreement with the regular course of nature. It is true that, perhaps, not an hour of the day was permitted to pass which did not, in some way or other, furnish new materials for the formation of his mind. But it was impossible for the materials thus collected to assume the form and figure even of the most inconsiderable organic whole. All was mingled together in one disorderly, scattered, and party-coloured mass of hundreds and thousands of partial representations and fragments of thought, huddled together, above and below, and by the sides of each other, without any apparent connexion or design. If thus the vacant tablets of his mind were soon enough superscribed, they were, at the same time, but too soon filled and disfigured with things which, in part, at least, were worthless and prejudicial. The unaccustomed impressions of the light and of the free air; the strange and often painful minglings of diverse excitatives which continually flowed in upon his senses; the effort to which his mind was constantly stimulated by his thirst for knowledge, labouring, as it were, to go beyond itself, to fasten upon, to devour, and to absorb into itself, whatsoever was new to him,—and all was new to him—all this was more than his feeble body, and delicate, yet constantly excited, and even over-excited nerves could bear. From my first visit to Caspar, on the 11th of July, I brought with me the fullest conviction, which in its proper place I also endeavoured to impress upon the minds of others, that Caspar Hauser must needs either die of a nervous fever, or be visited with some attack of insanity or idiocy, if some change were not speedily made in his situation. In a few days my apprehensions were partly justified by what actually occured. Caspar Hauser became sick: at least he became so unwell that a dangerous illness was feared. The official statement of his physician, Dr. Osterhausen's opinion, which, on this occasion, was sent by him to the magistracy of the city, was to the following effect.

"The multifarious impressions which all at once rushed upon Caspar Hauser, after he had for years been buried alive in a dungeon, where he lived secluded from all mankind, and left to himself alone, and which did not operate upon him singly and successively, but in a mass and altogether; the heterogeneous impressions made upon him by the free air, by the light, and by the objects which surrounded him, all of which were new to him; the awakening of his mental individuality, his desire of learning and of knowing, as well as the change that was made in his manner of living, &c.; the operation of all these causes could but produce effects which would powerfully shake, and finally injure, the health of a person possessing so very great a share of nervous sensibility.—When I saw him again, I found him totally changed; he was melancholy, very much dejected, and greatly enfeebled. There appeared to exist a morbid elevation of his nervous excitability. The muscles of his face were affected with frequent spasms. His hands trembled so much that he was scarcely able to hold anything. His eyes were inflamed, they could not bear the light, and they gave him considerable pain when he attempted to read or to look at any object attentively. His hearing was so sensitive, that all loud speaking caused him violent pain; so that he could no longer endure the sound of music, of which he had heretofore been so passionately fond. He lost his appetite, became costive, complained of unpleasant sensations in his abdomen, and, upon the whole, he felt very unwell.—I felt very uneasy on account of the state of his health, and particularly so, partly because his unconquerable aversion to anything but bread and water rendered it impossible to administer medicines to him, and partly because it was to be feared, that even the most inactive remedies might operate too powerfully upon him in the very highly excited state of his nerves."

On the 18th of July, Caspar Hauser was released from his abode in the tower, and was committed to the domestic care and superintendence of Mr. Daumer, a professor of a gymnasium, distinguished equally for the excellent qualities of his mind and of his heart, who now took upon himself entirely the care of his education, and who had also hitherto paid a fatherly attention to his instruction, and to the formation of his mind. In the family of this man, consisting of the worthy mother and sister of his instructor, he found, in a manner, a compensation for the loss of those beings whom nature had given him, and of whom the wickedness of man had deprived him.

We may form some conception of the great crowds of persons to whose curiosity Caspar Hauser was exposed, from the circumstance, that the magistracy of Nuremberg found it necessary, as soon as Caspar had been committed to the care of Professor Daumer, to insert the following notice in the public journals:—

"The homeless Caspar Hauser, has, in order to promote the development of the powers of his mind and body, been committed, by the magistracy of the city of Nuremberg, to the care of a particular instructor, who is well qualified to undertake that office. That both of them may be freed from any interruption in the pursuit of this object, and that Caspar Hauser may be able to enjoy that tranquillity which, in every respect, he so much needs, his instructor has been directed not to allow any more visits to Hauser for the future.

"The public in general, are therefore hereby duly informed thereof; so that all may avoid the mortification of being refused admittance to him: and it is also notified, that pertinacious importunity in insisting upon admittance to him, will, if necessary, be resisted by the assistance of the police."*

At Professor Daumer's, Caspar Hauser was for the first time furnished, instead of the bag of straw upon which he had lain in the tower, with a proper bed, with which he seemed to be exceedingly pleased. He would often say, that his bed was the only pleasant thing that he had met with in the world; every thing else was very bad indeed.—It was only after he slept in a bed, that he began to have dreams. Yet these he did not at first recognise as dreams, but related them to his instructor,

* This notice, nevertheless, did not entirely produce the desired effect. As few strangers visit Nuremberg without going to see the grave of St. Sebaldus, the paintings on glass in the church of St. Lawrence, &c so no one at that time, thought that he had fully seen the curiosities of Nuremberg, who had omitted to see the mysterious adopted child of that city. From the time of Caspar's arrival at Nuremberg, to the present moment, many hundreds of persons of almost all European nations, of every rank,—scholars, artists, statesmen, and officers of every description, as well as noble and princely personages, have seen and spoken with him.

when he awoke, as real occurrences. It was only at a later period that he learned to perceive the difference between waking and dreaming.*

One of the most difficult undertakings was to accustom him to the use of ordinary food, and this could be accomplished only by slow degrees, with much trouble and great caution.† The first that he was willing to take, was water gruel; which he learned to relish daily more and more, and on this account he imagined that it was every day made better and better; so that he would ask, what was the reason that it had not been made so good at first? Also all kinds of food prepared from meal, flour, and pulse, and whatever else bore a resemblance to bread, began soon to agree with him. At length, he was gradually accustomed to eat meat, by mixing at first only a few drops of gravy with his gruel, and a few threads of the muscular fibres of meat, of which the juices had been well boiled out, with

* These circumstances should not be left unnoticed by those who make the philosophy of the human mind their study; as they afford striking illustrations of the peculiar state of mind in which Caspar was at that time.

† Before he became accustomed to warm food, he felt a constant thirst; and he drank daily from ten to twelve quarts of water. But even yet, he is still a mighty water drinker.

his bread; and by gradually increasing the quantity.

In the notes respecting Caspar Hauser, which Professor Daumer has collected, he has made the following observations: "After he had learned regularly to eat meat, his mental activity was diminished; his eyes lost their brilliancy and expression; his vivid propensity to constant activity was subdued; the intense application of his mind gave way to absence and indifference; and the quickness of his apprehension was also considerably lessened." Whether this was really the effect of his feeding on meat, or whether this bluntness was not rather the consequence of the painful excess of excitement which preceded it, may very justly be questioned. We may, however, conclude, with much greater certainty, that the change of his diet, which was made by accustoming him to warm nourishment and to some animal food, must have had a very perceptible effect upon his growth. In Professor Daumer's house, he grew more than two inches in height in a very few weeks.

As the inflammation of his eyes, and the constant headache, with which every application of his eyesight was attended, made it impossible for him to read, write, or draw, Mr.

Daumer employed him in making pasteboard work, in which he very soon acquired considerable dexterity. He also taught him to play chess, which he soon learned, and practised with pleasure. Besides this, he was employed in easy garden-work, and made acquainted with the various productions, phenomena, and powers of nature; so that not a single day passed by which did not add something to his knowledge and make him acquainted with innumerable new objects of surprise, wonder, and admiration.

It required no little labour, and much patience, in correcting his mistakes, in order to teach him the difference between things which are, and such as are not, organized,—between animate and inanimate things; and between voluntary motion, and motion that is communicated from without. Many things which bore the form of men or animals, though cut in stone, carved in wood, or painted, he would still conceive to be animated, and ascribe to them such qualities as he perceived to exist in other animated beings. It appeared strange to him, that horses, unicorns, ostriches, &c., which were hewn or painted upon the walls of houses in the city, remained always stationary, and did not run away. He expressed his indignation against the statue in the garden belonging to the house in which he lived, because, although it was so dirty, yet it did not wash itself. When, for the first time, he saw the great crucifix on the outside of the church of St. Sebaldus, its view affected him with horror and with pain : and he earnestly entreated, that the man who was so dreadfully tormented might be taken down. Nor could he, for a long time, be pacified, although it was explained to him, that it was not any real man, but only an image, which felt nothing. He conceived every motion that he observed to take place in any object, to be a spontaneous effect of life. If a sheet of paper was blown down by the wind, he thought that it had run away from the table; and if a child's waggon was rolling down a hill, it was, in his opinion, making an excursion for its own amusement. He supposed that a tree manifested its life by moving its twigs and leaves; and its voice was heard in the rustling of its leaves, when they were moved by the wind. He also expressed his indignation against a boy who struck the stem of a tree with a small stick, for giving the tree so much pain. To judge from his expressions, the balls of a ninepin alley ran voluntarily along; they hurt other balls when they struck against them, and when they stopped it was because they were tired. Professor Daumer endeavoured for a long time, in vain, to convince him that a ball does not move voluntarily. He succeeded, at length, in doing so, by directing Caspar to make a ball himself, from the crumbs of his bread, and afterwards to roll it along. He was convinced that a humming-top, which he had long been spinning, did not move voluntarily, only by finding, that, after frequently winding up the cord, his arm began to hurt him; being thus sensibly convinced that he had himself exerted the power which was expended in causing it to move.

To animals, particularly, he for a long time ascribed the same properties as to men; and he appeared to distinguish the one from the other only by the difference of their external form. He was angry with a cat for taking its food only with its mouth, without ever using its hands for that purpose. He wished to teach it to use its paws, and to sit upright. He spoke to it as to a being like himself, and expressed great indignation at its unwillingness to attend to what he said, and to learn from him. On the contrary, he once highly commended the obedience of a certain dog. Seeing a grey cat, he asked, why she did not wash herself, that she might become white. When he saw oxen lying down on the pavement of the street, he wondered why they did not go home and lie down there. If it was replied that such things could not be expected from animals, because they were unable to act thus, his answer was immediately ready: then they ought to learn it; there were so many things which he also was obliged to learn.

Still less had he any conception of the origin and growth of any of the organical productions of nature. He always spoke as if all trees had been stuck into the ground; as if all leaves and flowers were the work of human hands. The first materials of an idea of the origin of plants, were furnished him by his planting, according to the directions of his instructor, a few beans with his own hands, in a flower-pot; and by his afterwards being made to observe how they germinated and produced leaves, as it were, under his own eye. But, in general, he was accustomed to ask, respecting almost every production of nature, who made that thing?

Of the beauties of nature he had no perception. Nor did nature seem to interest him otherwise than by exciting his curiosity, and by suggesting the question, who made such a thing? When, for the first time, he saw a rainbow, its view appeared for a few moments to give him pleasure. But he soon turned away from it; and he seemed to be much more interested in the question, who made it? than in the beauty of its appearance.

Yet there was one view which made a remarkable exception to this observation, and which must be regarded as a great, and never-to-be-forgotten incident, in the gradual development of his mental life. It was in the month of August, 1829, when, on a fine summer evening, his instructor shewed him, for the first time, the starry heavens. His astonishment and transport surpassed all description. He could not be satiated with its sight, and was ever returning to gaze upon it; at the same time accurately fixing with his eye the different groups that were pointed out to him, remarking the stars most distinguished for their brightness and observing the differences of their respective colour. "That," he exclaimed, "is, indeed, the most beautiful sight that I have ever yet seen in the world. But who has placed all those numerous beautiful candles there? who lights them? who puts them out?" When he was told, that, like the sun, with which he was already acquainted, they always continue to give light, he asked again, who placed them there above, that they may always continue to give light? At length, standing motionless, with his head bowed down, and his eyes staring, he fell into a train of deep and serious meditation. When he again recovered his recollection, his transport had been succeeded by deep sadness. He sank trembling upon a chair, and asked, why that wicked man had kept him always locked up, and had never shewn him any of these beautiful things? He (Caspar) had never done any harm. He then broke out into a fit of crying, which lasted for a long time, and which could with difficulty be soothed; and said that "the man with whom he had always been" might now also be locked up for a few days, that he might learn to know how hard it is to be treated so. Before seeing this beautiful celestial display, Caspar had never shown any thing like indignation against that man; and much less had he ever been willing to hear that he ought to be punished. Only weariness and slumber were able to quiet his sensations; and he did not fall asleep—a thing that had never happened to him before—until it was about 11 o'clock. Indeed, it was in Mr. Daumer's family that he began more and more to reflect upon his unhappy fate, and to become painfully sensible of what had been withheld and taken from him. It was only there, that the ideas of family, of relationship, of friendship,—of those human ties, that bind parents and children, and brothers and sisters to each other, were brought home to his feelings; it was only there that the names mother, sister, and brother were rendered intelligible to him, when he saw how mother, sister, and brother, were reciprocally united to each other by mutual affection, and by mutual endeavours to make each other happy. He would often ask for an explanation of what is meant by mother, by brother, and by sister; and endeavours were made to satisfy him by appropriate answers. Soon after, he was found sitting in his chair, apparently immersed in deep meditations. When he was asked, what was now again the matter with him? he replied with tears, " he had been thinking about what was the reason why *he* had not a mother, a brother, and a sister? for it was so very pretty a thing to have them." As the necessity of a state of perfect rest from all mental exertion was, at that time, particularly indicated by his extreme excitability, and, as exercise appeared absolutely necessary to strengthen his feeble frame, it was thought that, among other modes of exercise, riding on horseback might be highly beneficial to him, especially as he had taken a great fancy to it. As formerly wooden horses, so now living horses, had become his favourites. Of all animals, the horse appeared

H

to him to be the most beautiful creature; and whenever he saw a horseman managing his steed, his heart seemed to dilate with the wish, that he also might have such a horse under him. The riding master at Nuremberg, Mr. Rumpler, had the complaisance to gratify this longing; and he received Caspar among his scholars. Caspar, who, with the most intent watchfulness, observed everything that was said to him or to the other scholars, had, in the first lesson, not only imprinted the principal rules and elements of the art of riding upon his memory, but made them his own; so that in a few days, he had made such progress, that old and young scholars, who had been taking lessons for several months, were obliged to acknowledge, that he was vastly their superior. His seat, his courage, and his correct management of his horse, astonished every one; and he would undertake feats of horsemanship which, besides himself and his riding master, none dared to attempt. Once, when the riding master had been breaking in a fractious Turkish horse, he was so little alarmed at the sight, that he requested permission to ride that horse. After having exercised himself for some time, the boundaries of the riding school became too narrow for him; he longed to manage his horse in the open air; and here he displayed, besides great dexterity, an inexhaustible endurance, hardihood, and tenacity of body, which could not be equalled, even by those who were most inured to the exercise of riding. He was particularly fond of spirited and hard-trotting horses, and he often rode, for many hours together, without intermission, without fatigue, and without chafing or feeling the least uneasiness. One afternoon, he rode in a full trot from Nuremberg to the so-called old Veste and back again; and this feeble youth, who, about that time, would have been so much fatigued with walking a few miles in the city, as to be obliged to lie down quite exhausted, and go to bed a few hours sooner than usual, returned from performing this gigantic feat, apparently, as little fatigued as if he had only been walking his horse from one gate of the city to the other. This insensibility may, as Professor Daumer supposes, be chiefly owing to the fact, that he had been sitting for so many years upon a hard floor; which is, indeed, by no means improbable. Yet, besides this, we may, from Hauser's love of horses and his almost instinctive equestrian dexterity, be led to form the perhaps not altogether untenable conjecture, that by birth he must belong to a nation of horsemen. For, that abilities, which at first indeed were acquired artificially, but which have been sustained by practice throughout successive generations, may finally be propagated as natural propensities, and distinguished capacities for acquiring them, is not unknown; of which fact, the dexterity in swimming peculiar to the South-sea islanders, and the sharp-sightedness of the North American hunter-nations may serve as instances.

But when a certain sagacious policeman is induced, in consequence of Hauser's extraordinary equestrianism, to conjecture, that Caspar is probably a young English dragoon who has deserted from his regiment, in order to play off a trick on the good-natured inhabitants of Nuremberg on his own account, no one certainly will be inclined to dispute with the inventor for the honour of his hypothesis.

Besides his extraordinary equestrian talents, the extreme peculiarity, the almost preternatural acuteness and intensity of his sensual perceptions, appeared particularly remarkable in Caspar Hauser during his abode in Professor Daumer's house.

As to his sight, there existed, in respect to him, no twilight, no night, no darkness. This was first noticed by remarking that at night he stepped everywhere with the greatest confidence; and that, in dark places, he always refused a light when it was offered to him. He often looked with astonishment, or laughed, at persons who, in dark places, for instance, when entering a house, or walking on a staircase by night, sought safety in groping their way, or in laying hold on adjacent objects. In twilight, he even saw much better than in broad day light. Thus, after sunset, he once read the number of a house at a distance of one hundred and eighty paces, which, in daylight, he would not have been able to distinguish so far off. Towards the close of twilight, he once pointed out to his instructor a gnat that was hanging in a very distant spider's web. At a distance of certainly not less than sixty paces, he could distinguish the single berries, in a cluster of elderberries, from each other, and these berries from black currants. It has been proved by experiments carefully made, that in a perfectly dark night, he could distinguish different dark colours, such as blue and green, from each other.

When, at the commencement of twilight, a common eye could not yet distinguish more than three or four stars in the sky, he could already discern the different groups of stars, and he could distinguish the different single stars of which they were composed, from each other, according to their magnitudes, and the peculiarities of their coloured light. From the inclosure of the castle at Nuremberg, he could count a row of windows in the castle of Marloffstein; and from the castle, a row of the windows of a house lying below the fortress of Rothenberg. His sight was as sharp, in distinguishing objects near, as it was penetrating in discerning them at a distance. In dissecting plants, he noticed subtile distinctions and delicate particles which had entirely escaped the observation of others.

Scarcely less sharp and penetrating than his sight was his hearing. When taking a walk in the fields, he once heard, at a comparatively very great distance, the footsteps of several persons, and he could distinguish these persons from each other by their walk. He had once an opportunity of comparing the acuteness of his hearing with the still greater acuteness of hearing evinced by a blind man, who could distinguish even the most gentle step of a man walking barefoot. On this occasion he observed, that his hearing had formerly been much more acute; but that its acuteness had been considerably diminished since he had begun to eat meat; so that he could no longer distinguish sounds with so great a nicety as that blind man.

Of all his senses, that which was the most troublesome to him, which occasioned him the most painful feelings, and which made his life in the world more disagreeable to him than any other, was the sense of smelling. What to us is entirely scentless, was not so to him. The most delicate and delightful odours of flowers, for instance the rose, were perceived by him as insupportable stenches, which painfully affected his nerves.

What announces itself by its smell to others, only when very near, was scented by him at a very considerable distance. Excepting the smell of bread, of fennel, of anise, and of carraway, to which he says he had already been accustomed in his prison—for his bread was seasoned with these condiments—all kinds of smells were more or less disagreeable to him. When he was once asked, which of all other smells was most agreeable to him? he answered, "None at all." His walks and rides were often rendered very unpleasant by leading him near to flower gardens, tobacco fields, nut trees, and other plants which affected his olfactory nerves; and he paid dearly for his recreations in the free air, by suffering afterwards from headaches, cold sweats, and attacks of fever. He smelt tobacco, when in blossom in the fields, at the distance of fifty paces, and at more than one hundred paces, when it was hung up in bundles to dry, as is commonly the case about the houses in the villages near Nuremberg. He could distinguish apple, pear, and plum trees from each other at a considerable distance, by the smell of their leaves. The different colouring materials used in the painting of walls and furniture, and in the dying of cloths, &c., the pigments with which he coloured his pictures, the ink or pencil with which he wrote, all things about him, wafted odours to his nostrils which were unpleasant or painful to him. If a chimney-sweeper walked in the streets, though at the distance of several paces from him, he tnrned his face, shuddering from the smell. The smell of an old cheese made him feel unwell, and affected him with vomiting. The smell of strong vinegar, though fully a yard distant from him, operated so powerfully upon the nerves of his sight and smell, as to bring the water into his eyes. When a glass of wine was filled at table, at a considerable distance from him, he complained of its disagreeable smell, and of a sensation of heat in his head. The opening of a bottle of champaigne was sure to drive him from the table or to make him sick. What we call unpleasant smells were perceived by him with much less aversion, than many of our perfumes. The smell of fresh meat was, to him, the most horrible of all smells. When Professor Daumer, in the autumn of 1828, walked with Caspar near to St. John's church-yard, in the vicinity of Nuremberg, the smell of the dead bodies, of which the professor had not the slightest perception, affected him so powerfully, that he was immediately seized with an ague, and began to shudder. The ague was soon succeeded by a feverish heat, which at length broke out into a violent perspiration, by which his linen was thoroughly wet. He afterwards said, that he had never before experienced so great a heat. When, on his return, he came near to the city-gate, he said that he felt better; yet he complained that his sight had been obscured thereby. Similar effects were once experienced by him (on the 28th of September, 1828), when he had been for a considerable time walking by the side of a tobacco-field.

Professor Daumer first noticed the peculiar properties of Caspar's sense of feeling, and his susceptibility of metallic excitements, while he was yet at the tower. Here, a stranger once made him a present of a little wooden horse and a small magnet, with which, as the forepart of the horse was furnished with iron, it could be made to swim about in different directions. When Caspar was going to use this toy according to the instructions he had received, he felt himself very disagreeably affected; and he immediately locked it up in the box belonging to it, without ever taking it out again, as he was accustomed to do with his other playthings, in order to shew it to his visitors. When he was afterwards asked why he did so? he said, that that horse had occasioned him a pain which he had felt in his whole body and in all its members. After he had been removed to Professor Daumer's house, he kept the box with the magnet in a trunk; from which, in clearing out his things, it was accidentally taken and brought into notice. The idea was suggested thereby to Professor Daumer, who recollected the occurrence which had formerly taken place, to make an experiment on Caspar with the magnet belonging to the little horse. Caspar very soon experienced the most surprising effects. When Professor Daumer held the north pole towards him, Caspar put his hand to the pit of his stomach, and, drawing his waistcoat in an outward direction, said that it drew him thus; and that a current of air seemed to proceed from him. The south pole effected him less powerfully; and he said that it blew upon him. Professor Daumer and Professor Herrmann made, afterwards, several other experiments similar to these, and calculated to deceive him; but his feelings always told him very correctly, and even though the magnet was held at a considerable distance from him, —whether the north pole or the south pole was held towards him. Such experiments could not be continued long, because the perspiration soon appeared on his forehead, and he began to feel unwell.

In respect to his sensibility of the presence of other metals, and his ability to distinguish them from each other by his feelings alone, Professor Daumer has collected a great number of facts, from which I shall select only a few. In autumn, 1828, he once accidentally went into a shop filled with hardware, particularly with brass goods. He had scarcely entered, before he hurried out again, being affected with a violent shuddering, and saying that he felt a drawing in his whole body in all directions. —A stranger who visited him once slipt a piece of gold of the size of a kreutzer into his hand, without Caspar's being able to see it: he said immediately that he felt gold in his hand.—At a time when Caspar was absent, Professor Daumer placed a gold ring, a steel and brass compass, and a silver drawing pen, under some paper, so that it was impossible for him to see what was concealed under it. Daumer directed him to move his finger over the paper, without touching it; he did so; and by the difference of the sensation and strength of the attraction which these different metals caused him to feel at the point of his fingers, he accurately distinguished them all from each other, according to their respective matter and form.—Once, when the physician, Dr. Osterhausen, and the royal crown-fiscal, Brunner, from Munich, happened to be present, Mr. Daumer led Caspar, in order to try him, to a table covered with an oilcloth, upon which lay a sheet of paper, and desired him to say whether any metal was under it. He moved his finger over it, and then said, "There it draws!" " But, this time," replied Daumer, " you are, nevertheless, mistaken; for (withdrawing the paper) nothing lies under it." Caspar seemed, at first, to be somewhat embarrassed; but he put his finger again to the place where he thought he had felt the drawing, and assured them repeatedly, that he *there* felt a drawing. The oil-cloth was then removed, a stricter search was made, and a needle was actually found there. He described the feeling which minerals occasioned him as a kind of drawing sensation, which passed over him, accompanied, at the same time, with a chill which ascended, according as the objects were different, more or less up the arm; and which was also attended with other distinctive sensations. At the same time, the veins of the hand which had been exposed to the metallic excitation, were visibly swollen. Towards the end of December, 1828,—when the morbid excitability of his nerves had been almost removed,—his sensibility of the influence of metallic excitatives, began gradually to disappear, and was, at length, totally lost. Animal magnetism manifested itself in him in a manner equally surprising; and he retained his receptivity of it for a much longer time than he did that of metallic excitements. But, as the phenomena which appeared in Caspar, agree in all their essential characteristics with similar appearances in other well-known cases, it would be superfluous to add any other observations respecting them, than, that he always called his sensation of the streaming in upon him of the magnetic fluid, a blowing upon him. He experienced such magnetic sensations, not only when in contact with men, when they touched him with their hands, or when they, even at some distance, extended the points of their fingers towards him,

&c., but also when he was in contact with animals.

When he laid his hand upon a horse, a cold sensation, as he said, went up his arm; and when he was mounted, he felt as if a draught of wind passed through his body. But these sensations went off after he had several times rode his horse around the riding-school.

When he caught a cat by the tail, he was seized with a strong fit of shivering, and felt as if he had received a blow upon his hand. In March 1829, he was, for the first time, taken to a tent where foreign animals were exhibited, and, agreeably to his wish, he was placed in the third row of spectators. Immediately as he entered, he felt an ague, which was greatly increased when the rattle-snake was irritated and began to shake its rattles; and this was soon succeeded by a feverish heat and profuse perspiration. The eyes of the snake were not directed to the spot where he sat; and he maintains, that he was not conscious of any sensation of terror or of apprehension.

We now leave Caspar's physical and physiological aspect, in order to contemplate the interior region of his mind, which, while it exhibits to us the acuteness of his natural understanding, enables us at the same time to draw exact conclusions concerning the fate of his life, and the state of utter neglect in which his mind was left by the profligacy of human beings. Though his soul was filled with a childish kindness and gentleness, which rendered him incapable of hurting a worm or a fly, much less a man; though in his conduct in all the various relations of life, he showed that his soul was spotless and pure as the reflex of the eternal in the soul of an angel, yet, as we have already observed, he brought with him from his dungeon to the light of the world, not an idea, not the least presentiment of the existence of God, not a shadow of faith in any more elevated, invisible existence. Brought up like an animal, slumbering even while awake, sensible in the desert of his narrow dungeon only of the crudest wants of animal nature, occupied with nothing but the taking of his food and the eternal sameness of his wooden horses, the life of his soul could be compared only to the life of an oyster, which, adhering to its rock, is sensible of nothing but the absorption of its food, and perceives only the eternal uniform dashing of the waves; and in its narrow shell finds no room even for the most confined idea of a world without it. Still less was he capable of having the least presentiment of any thing that is above the earth, and above all worlds. Thus came Caspar, unswayed indeed by prejudices, but without any sense of what is invisible, incorporeal, and eternal, to this upper world, where, seized and driven around by the stunning vortex of external things, he was too much occupied with visible realities to suffer the want of any thing that is invisible to become perceptible to his mind. Nothing, at first, appeared to him to have any reality, but what he could see, hear, feel, smell, or taste; and his awakened, and soon also speculative understanding, would admit of nothing that was not based upon his sensual consciousness, that could not be placed within the reach of his senses, that could not be presented to him in the form of some coarse conception of his understanding sufficiently near to be brought home to him. All attempts made in the common way, to awaken religious ideas in his mind, were, for a long time, entirely fruitless. With great naiveté, he complained to Professor Daumer, that he did not know what the clergymen meant by all the things that they told him; of which he could comprehend nothing. In order somewhat to overcome his coarse material ideas, Professor Daumer endeavoured, in the following manner, to make him susceptible of some preparatory notions of the possibility to conceive and to believe the existence of an invisible world, and particularly the existence of God. Mr. Daumer asked him whether he had not thoughts, ideas, and a will. And when he acknowledged that he had, he asked him whether he could see them, hear them, &c.? When he said that he could not, he made him observe, that he was therefore conscious that there do exist things which we cannot see, nor otherwise perceive externally. Caspar acknowledged this; and he was much astonished at this discovery of the incorporeal nature of our interior being. Daumer continued: "A being that can think and will is called a spirit; God is such a spirit, and between him and the world there exists a relation, something like that between Caspar's thought and his body; as he, Caspar, can produce changes in his own body by his invisible thinking and willing, as he, for instance, can move his hands and feet, so God can produce changes in the world; he is the life in all things; he is the spirit that is operative in the whole world!" — Professor Daumer now ordered him to move his arm, and then asked him " if he could not, at the same time, lift and move the other arm?" " Certainly!" he replied. " Now, hence you see, then," continued Professor Daumer, "that your invisible thought and will, that is, your spirit, may be present and operative in two of your members at once, and, consequently, in two different places at the same time. The case is the same in respect to God; but on a grand scale: and now you may form some conception of what I mean by saying that God is everywhere present." Caspar testified great joy when this had been explained to him; and he said to his instructor, that what he had now told him was something "real;" whereas other people had never told him any thing upon that subject that was right. Yet instructions such as these, had, for a long time, no other effect than to render Hauser less refractory when the idea of God was presented to his mind; since thus a way was found, by which religious ideas could be instilled into him. But the apparently inborn Pyrrhonism of his nature, would nevertheless, on various occasions, break out anew in different forms and in different directions. He once asked, whether we might pray to God for any particular thing, and whether he would grant us what we prayed for; for instance, if he prayed to God to cure the malady of his eyes with which he was afflicted, would he do it? He was answered, that he was certainly permitted to pray; but that he must leave it to the wisdom of God to determine, whether it was proper that his prayer should be granted or not. "But," he replied, "I wish for the use of my eyes, that I may learn and work; and that must be good for me. God can have nothing against it." If he was then instructed that God has inscrutable reasons for refusing us even what most evidently appears to be good for us, in order, for instance, to try us, and to exercise our patience, such doctrines were always received by him coldly, and met with no acknowledgment. His doubts, questions, and objections, frequently embarrassed his instructor not a little; for instance, once when the conversation was concerning the omnipotence of God, he proposed the question: "Can Almighty God also make time recede?" a question which contained a bitter sarcastic allusion to the fate of his earlier life, and, in the back ground, concealed the inquiry, whether God could restore his childhood and youth, which had been lost to him in a living grave. From these few remarks we may infer, what was, in his mind, the state of positive religion, of christian dogmatics, of the doctrine of the atonement, and of similar doctrines, from stating his objections to which I willingly refrain.

There were two orders of men to whom Caspar had, for a considerable time, an unconquerable aversion—physicians and clergymen: to the first, " on account of the abominable medicines which they prescribed, and with which they made people sick;" and to the latter, because, as he expressed himself, they made people afraid, and confused them with incomprehensible stuff. When he saw a minister, he was seized with horror and dismay. If he was asked the cause of this, he would reply, " Because these people have already tormented me very much. Once, when I was at the tower, four of them came to me all at once, and told me things which at that time I could not at all comprehend; for instance, that God had created all things out of nothing. When I asked them for an explanation, they all began to cry out at the same time, and every one said something different. When I told them, All these things I do not yet understand; I must first learn to read and write; they replied, These things must be learned first. Nor did they go away, until I signified to them my desire, that they would at length leave me at rest." In churches, therefore, Caspar felt by no means happy. The crucifixes which he saw there, excited a horrible shuddering in him; because, for a long time, he involuntarily ascribed life to images. The singing of the congregation seemed to him as a repulsive bawling. "First," said he, after returning from attending a church, "the people bawl; and when they have done, the parson begins to bawl."

CHAPTER VII.

By the careful attention of Mr. Daumer's worthy family, by the use of proper exercise, and by the judicious employment of his time, Caspar Hauser's health had been greatly improved. He was diligent in learning, increased in knowledge, and made considerable progress in ciphering and writing; and he had proceeded so far in the latter, that, about the summer of 1829, he was able, at the desire of those who directed his actions, to collect his recollections of his life into a written memoir. This first attempt at an original exposition of his thoughts, although it could only be considered as a document exhibiting the retarded progress, and the consequent indigence and awkwardness of his still childish mind, was nevertheless viewed by him with the eyes of a young author when the first production of his pen is about to appear in print. This itch of authorship, caused this so-called history of his life, to be shown both to native and foreign visitors; and the story soon ran, and even appeared in several public journals, that Caspar Hauser was employed in writing a history of his life. It is highly probable that this very report occasioned the catastrophe which, soon after it was circulated, in the month of October, the same year (1829), was intended to bring his short life to a tragic end. Casper Hauser—if we may be permitted to indulge in conjectures—had at length become, to those who kept him secretly confined, a dangerous burthen. The child which they had so long fed, had become a boy, and was at length grown up to a young man. He became restless, his powers of life became more vivid, he sometimes made a noise, and it was necessary to keep him quiet by means of severe chastisement, of which he still bore fresh marks when he came to Nuremberg. Why they did not get rid of him in some other manner? Why they did not destroy him? Why as a child he had not been put out of the world? Whether it may not have been with instructions to murder him, that he was first delivered to his attendant, who, either from compassion, or with an intention to wait for times more favourable to the child who was to be made away with, or for other reasons, that may be imagined, had, at his own risk, kept the child alive and fed it! All this must be left to conjecture. However this may be, the time was come, or rather it was not come;

the secreted individual could no longer be kept concealed; it was necessary to get rid of him in some way or other, and—in a beggar's garb—he was sent to Nuremberg. It was intended that he should disappear there, either as a vagabond or as an idiot, in some public institution, or, if any attention was paid to the recommendation which he brought with him, as a soldier in some regiment. Contrary to every expectation, none of these events took place; the unknown foundling met with humane commiseration, and became the object of universal public attention; the public journals were filled with accounts of this mysterious young man, and with conjectures respecting him. From being the adopted child of the city of Nuremberg, for such the magistracy of the city had declared him, he became, at length, the child of Europe. The development of Caspar's mind is everywhere spoken of, marvellous things are related to the public of his progress, and now this human animal is writing a history of his life! He who gives a history of his life must be able to describe something relating to it.

Those persons, therefore, who had every reason to wish to remain in the darkness which they had drawn around themselves, and around all traces leading to them, could not but feel very uneasy at hearing of this intended autobiography.

The plan to bury poor Caspar alive in the waves of a world entirely unknown to him, had failed; and it was only now that Caspar's murder became, in the opinion of those who had committed this secret crime, in a manner, an act of self-defence.

Caspar was accustomed, between eleven and twelve o'clock, to go out of the house in order to attend a lesson in ciphering. But on Saturday, the 17th October, he was directed by his tutor to remain at home, because he felt unwell. About that hour, Professor Daumer took a walk; and, besides Caspar, who was known to be in his chamber, none remained at home but Daumer's mother, and his sister, who, about that time, was busy sweeping the house.

The house in which Casper lived, at Daumer's, lies in a distant and little-frequented part of the city, and is situated on an open place of an extraordinary size, which can scarcely be overlooked. The house, being built according to the ancient custom of Nuremberg, is very irregular and full of edges and corners, and consists of a front building, in which the landlord lived, and a back building in which Daumer's family resided. A narrow house-door leads, by a passage inclosing the yard on two sides, to the staircase belonging to Daumer's quarters; and, besides a wood-room, a place for poultry, and similar conveniences, there is in a corner, close under a winding staircase, a very low, small, and narrow water-closet. The small space in which this is, was rendered still smaller by a screen placed before it. Whoever is in the entry, upon a level with the ground (for instance, near the wood-room), is very well able to observe who comes down stairs and enters the water-closet.

About twelve o'clock the same day, when Professor Daumer's sister, Catherine, was busy sweeping the house, she observed, upon the staircase which leads from the first story to the yard, several spots of blood, and bloody footsteps, which she immediately wiped away, without, on that account, thinking that any thing extraordinary had happened. She supposed, that Caspar might have been seized on the staircase with a bleeding at the nose, and she went to his chamber to ask him about it. She did not find Caspar there; but she observed, also in his room, near the door, a few bloody footsteps. After she had again gone down stairs, in order to sweep also the above-mentioned passage in the yard, single traces of blood again met her eye, upon the stone-pavement of the passage. She went on to the water-closet where there lay a dense heap of clotted blood: this she shewed to the daughter of the landlord, who had just come to the spot, and who was of opinion that it was the blood of a cat. Daumer's sister, who immediately sponged the blood off, was now still more confirmed in the opinion, that Hauser had stained the staircase: he must have trod upon this clot of blood, and neglected to wipe his feet before he went up stairs. It was already past twelve o'clock; the table was spread; and Caspar, who at other times had always punctually come to dinner, stayed this time away. The mother of Professor Daumer, therefore, went down from her chamber to call Caspar, but was as unsuccessful in finding him as her daughter had been before her.

Mrs. Daumer was just in the act of going once more up into his chamber, when she was struck with observing something moist upon the cellar door which appeared to her like blood. Fearing that some misfortune had happened, she lifted up the cellar door; she observed upon all the steps of the cellar drops or large spots of blood; she went down to the lowest step; and she saw, in a corner of the cellar, which was filled with water, something white, glimmering at a distance. Mrs. Daumer then hurried back, and requested the landlord's servant-maid to go into the cellar, with a candle, to see what the white thing was that lay there. She had scarcely held the candle to the object pointed out to her, when she exclaimed, "There lies Caspar dead!" The servant-maid, and the son of the landlord, who in the meantime had come to their assistance, now lifted Caspar, who gave no signs of life, and whose face was pale as death and covered with blood, from the ground, and carried him out of the cellar. When he was brought up stairs, the first sign of life that he gave was a deep groan; and he then exclaimed, with a hollow voice, "Man! man!"—He was immediately put to bed; where, with his eyes shut, he, from time to time, cried out, or murmured to himself, the following words and broken sentences:—"Mother!—tell professor!—water-closet—man beat—black man, like sweep (kuchen)*—tell mother—not found in my chamber—hide in the cellar."

Upon this, he was seized with a severe ague, which was soon succeeded by violent

---

* This refers to a case in which Caspar had been very much frightened by the chimney-sweeper who was sweeping in the kitchen. The word kuchen probably meant küche—kitchen, which name he gave to the chimney-sweeper who, as mentioned above, had frightened him in the kitchen.

paroxysms, and finally by a complete frenzy, in which several strong men were scarcely able to hold him down. In these fits, he bit a considerable piece out of a porcelain cup, in which a warm draught had been brought him; and he swallowed it along with the potion. For nearly forty-eight hours, he remained in a state of perfect absence of mind. In his delirium, during the night, he uttered, from time to time, the following broken sentences: "Tell it to the burghermaster.—Not lock up.—Man away!—Man comes!—Away bell!—I to Furth ride down.—Not to Erlangen at the whale—not kill, not hold the mouth shut—not die!—Hauser, where been; not to Furth to-day; not more away; head ache already.—Not to Erlangen at the whale! The man kill me! Away! Don't kill! I all men love; do no one anything. Burghermaster's lady, help!—Man, I love you too; don't kill!—Why the man kill?—I have done you nothing.—Don't kill me! I will yet beg that you may not be locked up.—Never have let me out of my prison, you would even kill me! You should first have killed me, before I understood what it is to live. You must say why you locked me up," &c. Most of these sentences he repeated, mingled incoherently with each other.

The result of the inquiry instituted, with the assistance of the medical officer of the city jurisdiction, by the court of inquiry appointed by the judicial authorities,—to which the case was at length referred by the police court,—was as follows:

"The forehead of Hauser, who was lying in bed, was found to be hurt by a sharp wound in the middle of it, concerning the size and quality of which, the court's medical officer has given the following report, which was entered into the protocol.

"The wound is upon the forehead, about $10\frac{1}{2}$ lines from the root of the nose, running across it; so that two-thirds of the wound are on the right, and one-third of it on the left side of the forehead. The whole length of the wound, which runs in a straight line, is $19\frac{1}{2}$ lines.

"At present (October 20th) the edges of the wound are closed, and there scarcely remains an interstice of a quarter of a line between them. But this is somewhat broader at its left end than throughout the whole course of the wound; on which account it is to be presumed, that there it penetrated deepest. As far as regards the origin of the wound, it was evidently given to Hauser with a sharp cutting instrument, by a stroke or thrust (?). The sharp edges of the wound indicate the sharpness of the instrument's blade; the straightness of the wound indicates that it was occasioned by a stroke or thrust (?); because if the wound had been purely a cut, its beginning and end would have been more shallow and narrow, but the middle deeper; and on that very account it would appear more gaping. It is however most probable, that it was made by a stroke; because, if it had been made by a thrust, the adjoining parts would have been more bruised." The wound, as the physician declared, was in itself inconsiderable; any other person would have been cured of it in six days. But on account of the highly excited state of Caspar's nervous system, it was twenty-two days before he recovered from the consequences of it.

Caspar relates the substance of what happened, as follows:—" On the 17th I had been obliged to put off the ciphering lesson which I attended every day, at Mr. Erlangen's, from 11 to 12 o'clock; because, having an hour before received a walnut from Dr. Peru, I felt very ill; although I had not eaten more than a quarter of it. Professor Daumer, whom I informed of the circumstance, therefore told me, that I should not at this time attend my usual ciphering lesson, but remain at home.

Professor Daumer went out, and I retired to my chamber.

"I intended to employ myself in writing, but was prevented by indisposition from doing so, and compelled to go to the water-closet. While there, I heard a noise, like that which is usually heard when the door of the wood-room is opened, and which is well known to me; I also heard a soft sound of the house door bell; this did not however appear to proceed from ringing it, but from some immediate contact with the bell itself. Immediately after, I heard, softly, footsteps from the lower passage, and at the same time I saw, through the space between the screen before the private closet and the small staircase, that a man was sneaking through the passage. I observed the entirely black head of the man, and thought it was the chimney-sweeper. But when I was afterwards preparing to leave the narrow apartment in which I was, and my head was somewhat outside of it, the black man stood suddenly before me, and gave me a blow on the head; in consequence of which I immediately fell with my whole body on the ground." (Now follows a description of the man, which cannot well be communicated.) "Of the face and the hair of the man, I could perceive nothing, for he was veiled, and, indeed, as I believe, with a black silk handkerchief drawn over his whole head.

" After I had lain, probably for a considerable time, without consciousness, I came again to my senses. I felt something warm trickling down my face, and both of my hands, which I raised to my forehead, were, in consequence thereof, stained with blood. Frightened at this, I intended to run to mother*, but being seized with confusion and terror (for I was still afraid that the man who had struck me might attack me again), instead of reaching mother's door, I ran to the clothes-press before my room.† Here my sight failed me, and I endeavoured to keep myself upright by holding fast to the press with my hands.‡ When I had recovered, I wished again to go to mother's, but being still more confused, and straying still further, instead of going up stairs, I discovered, with horror, that I had come down stairs, and was again in the passage. The trap-door of the cellar was closed. Whence I got the strength to lift this heavy door, is, to this very moment, inconceivable to me. Ne-

* So he always called his foster-mother, the mother of Professor Daumer.

† Every step of Caspar's, which is mentioned in the above narrative, was found to be marked with bloody traces.

‡ The bloody marks upon the press were still visible for several days afterwards.

vertheless, I did lift it, and slipped down into the cellar.* By the cold water in the cellar, through which I was obliged to walk, I was restored to a more perfect state of consciousness. I observed a dry spot on the floor of the cellar, and I sat down upon it. I had scarcely sat down, when I heard the clock strike twelve. I then began to reflect: Here you are entirely forsaken, no one will look for you here.—This thought filled my eyes with tears, until I was seized with vomiting, and then lost my recollection. When I again regained my recollection, I found myself in my room upon the bed, and mother by my side."

In respect to the manner in which he was wounded, I (the author of this) cannot join in the opinion of the court.

I have several reasons, but which cannot with propriety be publicly made known, for believing that Caspar Hauser's wound was neither made by a stroke, nor by a thrust; neither with a sabre, with a hatchet, with a chisel, nor

* How true and naturally are the effects of terror and of fear here described!—That Caspar did not creep into the cellar through the open cellar-door, and that it was really necessary for him first to open it, is a matter of fact, which cannot be doubted; and it is equally true, that the opening of the cellar-door, which, to so feeble a person as Caspar, was a Herculean labour, would, at any other time, or in any other circumstances, have been quite impossible to him.

with a common knife made for cutting, but with another well-known sharp-cutting instrument; and that the wound was not aimed at the head, but at the throat; but (because, at the sight of the man, and of the armed fist which was suddenly extending itself towards his throat, Caspar instinctively stooped) that the blow glanced from his throat, which was protected by his chin, and was led upwards. The person who committed the act, may have thought, when Caspar immediately fell down bleeding, that it had fully succeeded; and he dared not to remain any longer by his victim, in order to examine whether it had fully succeeded or not, and in case it had not, to repeat the blow, because, on account of the situation of the place, he had every moment great reason to fear that he would be detected by somebody. Thus Caspar escaped with a wound on the forehead.

Other indications that might lead to the discovery of the person who had committed the act, soon appeared. Among others, for instance, it was ascertained, that, on the same day and in the same hour when the deed was done, the man described by Caspar, was seen to go out of Daumer's house; that, nearly about the same time, the same well-dressed person described by Caspar, was seen washing his hands (which were probably bloody), in a water-trough which stands in the street, not very far from Daumer's house; that about four days after the deed, a well-dressed gentleman, who wore clothes like those worn by the black man described by Hauser, went up to a low woman, who was going to the city, and questioned her earnestly concerning the life or death of the wounded Caspar; that he then went with this woman close to the gate, where a hand-bill was to be seen concerning Hauser's wound, which had been stuck up by the magistracy; and that he afterwards, without entering the city, absented himself in a very suspicious manner, &c.

But, if the reader's curiosity, or his love of knowledge, should inspire him with a wish to learn still more; if he should ask me what were the results of the judicial inquiries which were instituted; if he should desire to know to what tracks they have led, what spots were actually struck by the divining rod, and what was afterwards done; I shall be under the necessity of answering, that the laws, as well as the nature of the case, forbid the author to speak publicly of things which only the servant of the state can be permitted to know, or to conjecture. Yet I may allow myself to pronounce the assurance, that the judicial authorities have, with a faithfulness at once unwearied and regardless of consequences, endeavoured to prosecute their inquiries concerning the case, by the aid of all, even the most extraordinary means, which were at their disposal; and that their inquiries have not been altogether unsuccessful.

But not all heights, depths, and distances, are accessible to the reach of civil justice. And, in respect to many places in which justice might have reason to seek the giant perpetrator of such a crime, it would be necessary, in order to penetrate into them, to be in possession of Joshua's ram's horns, or at least of Oberon's horn, in order, for some time at least, to suspend the action of the powerful enchanted Colossuses that guard the golden gates of certain castles.

> But what is veiled in blackest shades of night,
> Must, when the morning dawns, be brought to light.

CHAPTER VIII.

If Caspar, who may now be reckoned among civilized and well-behaved men, were to enter a mixed company without being known, he would strike every one as a strange phenomenon.

His face, in which the soft traits of childhood are mingled with the harsher features of manhood, and a heart-winning friendliness with thoughtful seriousness, tinctured with a slight tinge of melancholy; his naiveté, his confidential openness, and his often more than childish inexperience, combined with a kind of sageness, and (though without affectation) with something of the gravity of a man of rank in his speech and demeanor; then, the awkwardness of his language, sometimes at a loss for words, and sometimes using such as have a harsh and foreign sound, as well as the stiffness of his deportment and his unpliant movements, —all these, make him appear, to every observant eye, as a mingled compound of child, youth, and man, while it seems impossible, at the first glance, to determine to which stage of life, this prepossessing combination of them all properly belongs.

In his mind, there appears nothing of genius; not even any remarkable talent ; what he learns he owes to an obstinately persevering application. Also the wild flame of that fiery zeal, with which in the beginning he seemed anxious to burst open all the gates of science, has long since been extinguished. In all things that he undertakes, he remains stationary, either at the commencement, or when arrived at mediocrity. Without a spark of fancy, incapable of uttering a single pleasantry, or even of understanding a figurative expression, he possesses dry, but thoroughly sound common sense, and in respect to things which directly concern his person, and which lie within the narrow sphere of his knowledge and experience, he shews an accuracy and an acuteness of judgment, which might shame and confound many a learned pedant.

In understanding a man, in knowledge a little child, and, in many things, more ignorant than a child, the whole of his language

* Except for horsemanship, of which he was always passionately fond. In managing his horse, as well as in mounting and dismounting with dexterity and elegance, he equals the most skilful riding-master. To many of our most distinguished officers, Caspar is, in this respect, an object of admiration.

and demeanor shows often a strangely contrasted mingling of manly with childish behaviour. With a serious countenance, and in a tone of great importance, he often utters things, which, coming from any other person of the same age, would be called stupid or silly; but which, coming from him, always forces from us a sad compassionate smile. It is particularly farcical to hear him speak of the future plans of his life; of the manner in which, after having learned a great deal and earned money, he intends to settle himself with his wife, whom he considers as an indispensable part of domestic furniture.

He never thinks of a wife in any other manner than as a housekeeper, or as an upper servant, whom a man may keep as long as she suits him, and may turn away again, if she frequently spoils his soup, and does not properly mend his shirts, or brush his coats, &c.

Mild and gentle, without vicious inclinations, and without passions and strong emotions, his quiet mind resembles the smooth mirror of a lake in the stillness of a moonlight night. Incapable of hurting an animal, compassionate even to the worm, which he is afraid to tread upon, timid even to cowardice*, he will nevertheless act regardless of consequences, and

* Particularly since the attempt made to murder him.

even without forbearance, whenever, according to his own convictions, it becomes necessary to defend or to execute purposes which he has once perceived and acknowledged to be right. If he feels himself oppressed in his situation, he will long bear it patiently, and will endeavour to get out of the way of the person who is thus troublesome to him, or will endeavour to effect a change in his conduct by mild expostulations; but, finally, if he cannot help himself in any other manner, as soon as an opportunity offers of doing so, he will very quietly slip off the bonds that confine him, yet without bearing the least malice against him who may have injured him. He is obedient, obliging, and yielding; but the man that accuses him wrongfully, or asserts to be true what he believes to be untrue, need not expect, that, from mere complaisance, or from other considerations, he will submit to injustice or to falsehood; he will always modestly, but firmly, insist upon his right; or, perhaps, if the other seems inclined obstinately to maintain his ground against him, he will silently leave him.

As a mature youth who has slept away his childhood and boyhood, too old to be considered as a child, and too childishly ignorant to be regarded as a young man; without companions of an equal age; without country, and without parents and relations; as it were the only being of his kind—every moment reminds him of his solitude amidst the bustle of the world that presses upon him; of his weakness, feebleness, and inability to combat against the power of those contingencies that rule his fate; and, above all, of the dependance of his person upon the favour or disfavour of men. Hence, his expertness in observing men, which was almost forced upon him by the necessity of self-defence; hence the circumspect acuteness which, by ill-disposed persons, has been called slyness and cunning—with which he quickly seizes their peculiarities and foibles, and knows how to accommodate himself to those who are able to do him good or harm, to avoid offences, to oblige them, adroitly to make known to them his wishes, and to render the good-will of his favourers and friends serviceable to him. Neither childish tricks and wanton pranks, nor instances of mischief and malice, can be laid to his charge; for the first, he possesses too much cool deliberation and seriousness, and for the latter, he possesses too much good nature, combined with a love of justice, by the dictates of which he regulates his conduct with a scrupulous exactness, which, without affectation, approaches even to pedantry.

One of the greatest errors committed in the education of this young man, and in the formation of his mind, was evidently, that, instead of forming his mind upon the model of common humanity suited to his individual peculiarities, he was sent a year or two ago to the gymnasium, where he was besides made to commence in a higher class.* This poor neglected youth, who, but shortly before, had for the first time cast a look into the world, and who was still deficient in so much knowledge which other children acquire at their mother's breast, or in the laps of their nurses, was at once obliged to torment his head with the Latin grammar and Latin exercises; with Cornelius Nepos, and, finally, even with Cæsar's Commentaries.

Screwed into the common form of school education, his mind suffered as it were its second imprisonment. As formerly, the walls of his dungeon, so now, the walls of the schoolroom excluded him from nature and from life; instead of useful things he was made to learn

* From this situation he has, however, since I have been writing this small work, been delivered by the generosity of the noble Earl Stanhope, who has formally adopted him as his foster-son.

He lives now at Anspach, where he has been just put under the care of an able school-master, who has taken him into his house. Some time hence he will, under safe conduct, follow his beloved foster-father to England.

words and phrases, the sense of which, and their relation to things and conceptions, he was unable to comprehend; and thus, his childhood was, in the most unnatural manner, lengthened. While he was thus wasting his time, and his sufficiently scanty mental powers, upon the dry trash of a grammar school, his mind continued to starve, for want of the most necessary knowledge of things which might have nourished and exhilarated it, which might have given him some indemnification for the loss of his youth, and might have served as a foundation for some useful employment of his time in future. "I do not know"—he would often say with vexation, and almost in despair —"I do not know what good all these things are to do me, since I neither can nor wish to become a clergyman." When once a pedant said to him, "The Latin language is indispensably necessary for the sake of the German language; in order to have a thorough knowledge of the German, it is necessary to learn the Latin;" his good sense replied; "Was it then necessary for the Romans to learn German, in order to have a thorough knowledge of how they were to speak and write Latin?"

We may judge how the Latin suited Caspar, and Caspar the Latin, from the circumstance, that when this bearded Latinist was staying with me for a short time in the spring of 1831, he had not yet learned by experience, that objects of sight appear smaller at a distance than they really are. He wondered that the trees of an alley in which we were walking became smaller and lower, and the walk narrower at a distance; so that it appeared as if at length it would be impossible to pass them. He had not observed this at Nuremberg, and when he had walked down the alley with me, he was astonished, as if he had been looking upon the effects of magic, to find that each of these trees were equally high, and that the walk was everywhere equally broad.

The oppressive consciousness of his ignorance, helplessness, and dependance; the conviction that he should never be able to regain his lost youth, to equal those who were of the same age with him, and to become a useful man in the world; that, not only had the most beautiful part of man's life been taken away from him, but that also the whole remainder of his life had been crippled and rendered wretched; and, finally, that, besides all this, the miserable remainder of his respited life, was every moment threatened by a secret enemy, by the dagger of an assassin;—these are the pitiable contents of the tale which is told by the clouds of grief which overhang his brow, and, not unfrequently, pour themselves forth in tears and in sorrowing lamentations.

During the time he was staying at my house, I often took him along with me in my walks, and I conducted him once, on a pleasant morning, up one of our, so-called, mountains, where a beautiful and cheerful prospect opens upon the handsome city lying beneath it, and upon a lovely valley surrounded by hills. Caspar was, for a moment, highly delighted with the view; but he soon became silent and sad.

To my question concerning the reason of his altered humour, he replied, "I was just thinking how many beautiful things there are in the world, and how hard it is for me to have lived so long and to have seen nothing of them; and how happy children are who have been able to see all these things from their earliest infancy, and can still look at them. I am already so old, and am still obliged to learn what children knew long ago. I wish I had never come out of my cage; he who put me there should have left me there. Then I should never have known and felt the want of any thing; and I should not have experienced the misery of never having been a child, and of having come so late into the world." I endeavoured to pacify him by telling him, "That in respect to the beauties of nature, there was no great cause for regretting his fate in comparison with that of other children and men who had been in the world since their childhood. Most men, having grown up amidst these glorious sights, and considering them as common things which they see every day, regard them with indifference; and, retaining the same insensibility throughout their whole life, they feel no more at beholding them, than animals grazing in a meadow. For him (Caspar) who had entered upon life as a young man, they had been preserved in all their freshness and purity; and hereby no small indemnification was given him for the loss of his 'earlier years; and he had thus gained a considerable advantage over them." He answered nothing, and seemed, if not convinced, yet somewhat comforted. But it will never be possible, at any time, entirely to comfort him respecting his fate. He is a tender tree, from which the crown has been taken, and the heart of whose root is gnawed by a worm.

In such states of mind, and thus feeling his situation, religion, faith in God, and a hope in Providence founded upon that faith, could not but find entrance into a heart so much in need of comfort. He is now, in the true sense of the word, a pious man; he speaks with devotion of God, and is fond of reading books of rational edification. But, to be sure, he would swear to none of the symbolical books; and much less would he feel happy in a devout assembly of the disciples of Hengstenberg and his company.*

Taken by times away from the nursery-tales of his early attendants, buried as a child, and raised again to life as a ripe young man, he brought with him to the light of the world, a mind freed from every kind of superstition. As at first it was with difficulty that he could be made conscious of the existence of his own spirit, he is in nowise inclined to believe in ghosts or hobgoblins. He laughs at the belief of spectral apparitions, as at the most inconceivable of all human absurdities; he fears nothing but the secret enemy whose murderous steel he has felt; and, if security could be given him, that he had nothing to dread from that man, he would walk any hour of the night over a churchyard, and sleep, without apprehension, upon graves.

His present mode of life is that which is common to most men. With the exception of pork, he eats all kinds of meats that are not

* He was educated in the Evangelical-Lutheran religion, which most of the inhabitants of Nuremberg profess.

seasoned with hot spices. His favourite condiments are still carraway, fennel, and coriander. His drink continues to be water; and only in the morning, he takes a cup of unspiced chocolate instead of it. All fermented liquors, beer, and wine, as also tea and coffee, are still an abomination to him; and, if a few drops of them were forced upon him, they would infallibly make him sick.

The extraordinary, almost preternatural elevation of his senses, has also been diminished, and has almost sunk to the common level. He is indeed still able to see in the dark; so that, in respect to him, there exists no real night but only twilight; but he is no longer able to read in the dark, nor to recognize the most minute objects at a great distance. Whereas he was formerly able to see much better and more distinctly in a dark night than by day-light, the contrary is now the case. Like other men, he is now able to bear, and he loves, the light of the sun, and it no longer distresses his eyes. Of the gigantic powers of his memory, and of other astonishing qualities, not a trace remains. He no longer retains any thing that is extraordinary, but his extraordinary fate, his indescribable goodness, and the exceeding amiableness of his disposition.

APPENDIX,

CONTAINING

FURTHER DETAILS,

By G. F. DAUMER,

Professor of a Gymnasium, and formerly Caspar's Foster father:

AND

CONJECTURES

RESPECTING CASPAR HAUSER'S PLACE OF CONFINEMENT, &c. &c.

By M. SCHMIDT VON LÜBEC,

Knight of the Dane Broge at Altona.

FURTHER DETAILS,
By G. F. DAUMER.

Caspar Hauser's Visit to the Theatre.

WHEN taken to the theatre in September and October, 1828, he was only struck with the splendid dresses of the performers; of what was said by them he understood nothing; but it was from them that he first began to comprehend and understand what was spoken in the way of conversation or dialogue. If a comic character were introduced, it excited his aversion rather than his laughter, and he longed for its disappearance; for what was comic and ludicrous gave him at first no pleasure, and what is considered by us amusing, was to him offensive and disgusting. In October he went to hear Pasiello's Opera of " The Miller's Wife," but he took the precaution to provide himself with some cotton to stop his ears during the performance of the forte parts, otherwise he would not at this time have been able to have enjoyed the captivating music of the Opera.

The regimentals of the Baron (a character in the Opera) afforded him great pleasure, but he manifested the greatest abhorrence of the Steward, especially of his bag-wig; his curls were most offensive to him, even more so, he said, than a beard, and he often asked why they were not cut off.* The presence of this Steward was so intolerable to him, that he frequently turned away his head, and took offence when he appeared, but he testified much satisfaction when he withdrew. He was surprised at this "odious fellow's" familiarity with the other "fine persons," and wondered that they would converse with him.

When the Steward brought out the Baron's clothes from the chamber, he was displeased at their being even touched by the "hateful man;" and when, on some occasion, the Baron threatened a notary with his sword, he said, that he ought rather to run the "hateful fellow" through. This was the first expression of the kind I had ever heard from him; and the sensation he felt at the time must have

---

* When he came to my house he wished to cut off the whiskers of the cat. Beards, curls, long hair, and whiskers, were his aversion; and he sometimes shuddered excessively at the sight of them.

been similar to that experienced when we are inclined to annihilate an odious insect.

After the performance at the Opera, he spoke of " the odious man," with a distortion of countenance as if he were about to take an emetic.

The Impression made on Caspar by a Storm.

He was at first in an excessively painful condition during the continuance of a storm; and in May, 1829, I noticed still, on such an occasion, a convulsive motion in his countenance and limbs; an appearance which, at that time, was not common. He felt an internal chill, with frequent shiverings and shudderings; and said, that during a storm it was just as if every thing in his body were loose and in motion, and he felt a pressure from above his head downwards. The chill was most intense on the left side.* He was obliged involuntarily to shut his eyes by pressing them, and he trembled greatly. The chill continued until the storm was over; and in the middle of his breast he felt a *place* (or spot) quite cold, and which appeared to him as if it were altogether loose. The pressure increased in proportion

* His left side I found, on all occasions, to be the weaker and more diseased.

to the violence of the thunder. At the lightning he felt a pain in his eyes, as from the pricking of needles; and, about half an hour after, a bleeding at his nose came on, which relieved his head. By his own feelings he could tell whether the storm would be of short or of long continuance. If it were to last a short time, the coldness of his hands and feet was more like the temperature of the rest of his body; but they became very cold—much colder than the other parts of his body, when it continued a long while. At the end of July, 1829, a storm no longer made any impression on him; but the attempted assassination again excited this feeling in him; and in the summer, 1830, previous to a storm he felt a burning heat in a healed shot-wound, which he had once accidentally given to himself.

I adjoin to these remarks the following from the pen of Hauser himself, just as he wrote them down.

"As I heard in a former year (1828) the first storm, I describe what an odd impression and effect it produced upon me. Half an hour before the storm I felt a very great chill, so that I could no longer play on the musical glasses; I must lie down and cover myself, but still I could not make myself warm. The chill very likely lasted a quarter of an hour; afterwards

I felt a great heat and pain in my whole body, especially in my head; I stood up, went back to the horses, and considered why they did not carry me home, and always plagued me so.* All at once it begins to thunder; I am very much frightened, as I have felt a painful pressure. I began to cry, sat myself down in the corner, kept there quite still. Then mother† came, asked me why I cried; I said, ' Mother, me go home.'‡ Then she said, ' Me should not dare to go out just then, there is a great man outside who is very angry.' I beckoned out of the window, and she said to me, ' If thou art not brave, then he is angry!' I gave for an answer, 'I truly brave.' She wished to go away; I let her not go. I told mother to remain there; then said she, ' He is not angry with thee, only with such children as are always in the street.' When it has thundered I always stooped down; then said she, ' Caspar, be not afraid, I certainly remain

---

* He regarded all the pain which he experienced as an evil brought upon him by man, or much rather the world of men in which he then lived, appeared to him as an unfriendly and mischievous being, from whom he wished to escape.

† The gaoler's wife, whom he called *mother* at that time.

‡ He told me that at that time he understood the meaning of those words which the keeper of the prison had explained, and really by them he had wished to express his desire to return to his dungeon

with thee.' I gave her for answer, 'This man shall also leave off quarrelling with the others —I certainly tell Julie* that he shall be brave.' When it thundered it has given me a very painful pressure upon the head, as if some one had struck me on the head with the hand; afterwards, also, it gave me a slight shivering, as if it had frozen me very much. The storm lasted nearly an hour : when it was gone away, after a few minutes, I felt a little heat; this lasted a long time; then a shivering is given to me; then the pains in the body were away; but I felt the head-ache more violent. It was a long time after the storm before I lost my head-ache: it gave me again such a shuddering. Then said I, as the storm was gone by, ' Mother, now you say that the man shall not be angry any more ; also tell Julie he shall no more be naughty.' Then said she, 'I tell the man he shall no more be angry.'"

Written in the year 1829.—" On the 7th of August there came a storm ; this has produced a wonderful effect. A quarter of an hour before the storm it had given me a little shivering, as if a frost would fall upon me; then it was on my breast as if any one had bound me very tight; then I felt a sort of giddiness in

* This means, I will certainly inform Julius of it. He meant the son of the keeper of the prison.

my head; this has lasted till the storm was past away. Then I felt so light in my whole body—then again it has given me a little shivering; since this, it was every day more trifling.

"Now I can say, for the first time, what sort of a feel I had in the former summer. I have always said that I was so afraid, while I did not understand it, that I always felt more fear on that day than on other occasions; therefore, I have been so terrified when a storm comes on."

Effect produced by the Moon.

He saw the moon, for the first time, while at my house, in 1828. It was quite full moon. On the day before he had felt worse than usual, probably the consequence of the approaching full moon. After contemplating it, his indisposition became more violent, particularly the oppression on his breast. He continued in the same state the following day, but it afterwards went off. If he looked at the moon more than *cursorily*, his whole body was chilled, and emotions of horror were observable in him. This was particularly the case with him during the very warm season of the year, at the beginning of August or later;

and once in October when he looked at the full moon from a warm room in which he had long been. His assurances, from subsequent recollections, are the following:—When the moon was visible he was much more indisposed than when it could not be seen: when the moon, according to his own expression, was like a bow, his shivering was not so strong: when it was a half moon, not half so strong; but when it was quite full, his chill and other sensations, respecting which he expressed himself too indistinctly for me to ascertain anything clearly, were the strongest. After gazing on it for a long time he had a very violent burning in his eyes, and every thing appeared white to him; this, however, may be ascribed to the usual excitement of light. By the operations of the stars no remarkable effect was produced upon Hauser. When I told him to fix his eyes on the stars, and asked him if he felt any effect from them, he affirmed that he did not.

Hauser and his Cat.

Hauser, before he had learned to relish meat, in 1828, was on good terms with a cat which had been brought up in my house. This cat, indeed, allowed herself to be touched and brought into the apartment; but never by any one, when she was at liberty. On the contrary, whenever Hauser came into the garden she ran to him, if other persons did not frighten her away, suffered herself to be caught and carried about by him, and chased with him in play around the garden. She caressed his feet, which, he said, caused him a very pleasing sensation of a peculiar kind.* This cat ate nothing but flesh and milk, and would not eat dry bread even when very hungry; but out of Hauser's hand she would eat it readily, and fruit as well. I once offered her some boiled apple, which she smelt, but allowed to remain untouched: Hauser then took it in his hand and offered it to her, upon which she devoured it immediately. Once she came to Hauser, who was in the garden, with a long ribbon that she had found somewhere, and ran close to him, to make him perceive that she wished to play with him.† I once saw the cat, as she perceived Hauser come into the garden, look for the ribbon, spring into the hedge and come back with it.

Hauser maintained that this animal first ceased to follow him about as usual, when he

* This, as it appears, was the only animal magnetic effect at that time which was beneficial to him.

† Hauser had previously played frequently with her with a garter.

began to relish meat.* He himself wrote the following on this subject in his own peculiar manner.

"Mr. Professor Daumer had a cat which had white and black spots.† With her I amused myself many hours in the garden. One morning I went into the garden and thought, now if the cat were in the garden, I would play with her to-day very gladly. As I came back to the garden door she immediately ran to meet me; I called to her, 'Puss, art thou there indeed,' and ran away towards the end of the garden, but she could run better than I, and I ran not quite to the other end, but turned round and wished to go back to mother to have a ribbon given to me that I might have a good bit of play with her; when I went slowly downwards, she ran before me and sprang into the field and brought a ribbon to me, and I played with it half an hour long; then came Mr. Professor and he would see how I played with her; then Mr. Professor at first looked out of the window, and as he could not

* By means of eating animal food, *the magnetic* and *somnambulistic* qualities, in the nature of Hauser were suppressed for a long time. The former returned in consequence of the attempt to murder him.

† Hauser, according to the custom of the uneducated, introduces into his narrative, circumstances which are quite unimportant and unessential.

see downwards very well, he also came into the garden, but as soon as he opened the garden door, the cat left off playing with me and ran away out of the garden. I did not know exactly why the cat ran away out of the garden to-day, and did not first give me the signal that she could not play with me any longer, she ran no longer after the ribbon, but back to my feet, with which she played a long time, and then made a little cry and went away quite slowly to the garden door."

Sundry Remarks by Hauser himself.

The course which was taken for the development of Hauser's intellectual faculties may be easily gathered from the essays which are in my possession, written by himself. In the autumn of 1828, I allowed him to prepare some trifling remarks on pleasing subjects, which might tend to improve him. Two or three of these, which I give here, are the first which he put in a written form, and they shew him to be quite the child.

1. " Yesterday, the Lord Baron von Schœurl brought me a costly ring, that I hitherto have not had any pleasure so great as yesterday; and this ring shall be a keep-sake as long as I live, so I forget not the Lord Baron von

Schœurl as he has given me such a beautiful keep-sake."

2. " Yesterday, I have been out on Peterheide, where I have seen a great many men, and many other things, and also some monkeys which have done very many tricks; but these are odious beasts. And I have also seen some dogs which have learned dances and have worn fine clothes, they have been right beautiful."

3. " Several weeks ago, I have seen my name in garden cress, and this has been right beautiful; this has made me so much joy that I cannot tell it; then into the garden, which has many pears, come some one who has trodden down my name. Then I cried to Mr. Professor, I said I shall make it again, I have made it the other morning, but the cats have trodden it down again."

I also caused him, in 1828, to write a history of his fate. Of this, as he then generally was accustomed to leave his remarks incomplete, there are many commencements in my hands. The first is to this effect.

" The History of Caspar Hauser, I myself will write how hard it has gone with me. There, where I always was shut up in that prison, there it was always right well with me while I knew nothing of the world, and so long as I was shut up and had never seen any man. I have had two wooden horses and a dog, with these I always have played, but I cannot tell whether I have played with them all the day long or not, as I knew not what a day or a night is, and I will describe it as it has appeared in the prison; there was straw therein," &c. &c. &c.

The following is another beginning:—" This history of Caspar Hauser will I write myself. How I have lived in the prison, and describe how it appeared, and all that happened to me therein," &c. &c.

Of a third attempt, of February, 1829, in which there appears, indeed, a more polished, but still a very natural and ingenuous style of composition, the following is a fragment:—

" This narrative of my life and my former situation is written from recollection.

" The prison in which I was obliged to live until my release, was, perhaps, six or seven feet long, four broad, and five high. On the side there were two little windows shut (or closed) with wood which looked very black.*

* With regard to the acception of the expression, that it was wood which he had seen, either in or before the window, was given to Hauser by others. He merely mentions the cross-barred form and the black colour.

On the ground there was laid some straw on which I used to eat and sleep. My legs were covered from the knee with a rug or mat. Near my bed, on the left side, on the ground, there was a hole and a vessel in it*: there was also a lid over it, which I was obliged to push aside and always covered it again. The dress which I wore was a shirt and short trowsers, but without any back-part, as I could not undo them. I had the trowsers on my bare body: the shirt was on the outside. My food was only water and bread. I was sometimes in want of water: bread was always sufficient there. I had two wooden horses and a dog; with them I always amused myself. I had ribbons of red and blue colour, with which I decked the horses and the dog; but many times they fell down, so that I could not find them. When I awoke the piece of bread lay near me, and a little pitcher of water. At first I seized the water to quench my thirst, then I ate the

* This and other circumstances, which are of importance for determining the affair (for example, whether *Hauser* was fastened to the ground, and could not turn round), were first discovered by the very pertinent inquiries which were made of Hauser in my house by my friend Professor Hermann of Munich, when he was at Nuremberg in 1828. It was so difficult at first to understand him, that a great deal of misconception and incomprehension was necessarily the consequence, but which was all removed by the persevering inquiries and observations of that gentleman and myself.

bread; after this I took the horses and dressed them a long time; then I took the dog. When I had done with it, I drank the remaining water, and took the two horses once again, pulled off all the ribbons, and dressed them afresh, and past a long time in this manner. Then I ate the bread; I also wished to drink, but there was no longer any water there. Then I took the dog and wished to dress it like the horses, but I could no longer satisfy myself with it, as my mouth was so very dry. *I often took the little pitcher in my hand and held it long to my mouth, but there came out no water. I always put it down again, and waited a long time to see if the water could come again,* as I had not any notion that the water must be brought to me; I had not even a notion that there could be any person but me; but when I had waited a long time and no water came, then I laid myself on my back and fell asleep. I awoke again, and then I did as at first, that is, stretch out my hand for the water, and as often as I awoke there was always water in the little pitcher; then it was well with me. I took the horses again and did immediately again what I have related already. Commonly I found the water right good, but many times it was not so good, and when I had drank it, I lost all liveliness, and also did not play, I only slept.* When I awoke it was as bright at one time as at another. I have never seen such bright daylight as that in which I now live; but the first time that the man came to me, he placed quite a low stool before me, laid a piece of paper and a lead pencil on it, then he took my hand, put the pencil into it, pressed my fingers together, and wrote something for me. That he did very often until I could do like it. This he shewed me how to do seven or eight times: *it pleased me very much, as it appeared black and white.* Then he left my hand at liberty to write all alone. I wrote on, and did it according as he had shewn me, and repeated this often," &c. &c. &c.

Hauser's first entrance into Nuremberg described by himself.

As a proof of Hauser's written declarations, I give the following remarkable narrative, which I have allowed him to append to my remarks, and of which I adduce a few passages. It would be difficult for the most natural and profoundly crafty deceiver to compose anything which could possibly be equal to this.

* In consequence of the narcotic which had been infused into the cup.

Hauser's manner, &c. is closely imitated.

"I stood a long time in the above-mentioned place in which the man* had left me, until the other man† took my letter and conducted me to the house of the commandant. When I came to the house, I felt, from the loud voices which I heard, violent pains in my head. The officers placed me on a stool‡, but I could not answer with any words but those which I had learned, and these I made use of, without any distinction, to express fatigue and pain: thereupon he brought me a pewter plate with some meat, and beer in a glass. The brightness of the pewter, and the colour of the beer, pleased me, but soon the smell of the beer gave me pain. I thrust it away; he wished to force me, but I always pushed it back. Then he brought me some water and a piece of bread, which I knew again immediately, and took it in my hand and ate and drank.

"The water was so fresh and good, that I drank three or four glasses of it, and felt myself quite strengthened. Then he laid me in the stable, and I fell asleep as soon as I

* The unknown who had brought him to the city.

† The citizen who found him in the place where his unknown conductor had left him.

‡ Hauser can only recollect that the officer spoke to him and that he wished to interrogate him; which was undoubtedly the case.

was in it. When the commandant came home, I was awakened. I saw his uniform and his sword. I was astonished and delighted with it, and wished to have such a one. I said, *I möcht ah a söchana Reiter wern wie Voter is;* by which I meant to give him to understand that some one should give me such a beautiful shining thing. They began to speak, and so loud that it gave me pain in my whole body.* I began to cry, and said the same words. Then they took me to the police, and that was my most painful walk. When I came thither, there were very many men there; I was astonished, and knew not what that was that made them speak so continually and so loud: then they gave me snuff, which I was obliged to put into my nose, and that made me very ill, and I began to cry, as I felt frightful pain in my head. They teazed me also with all sorts of things which caused me shocking pain†, and I continued to weep

---

* Even in my house, he suffered greatly when any one addressed him in a loud key.

† Before Hauser was brought to the Burghermaster Binder, from whom he experienced the first kind treatment, the most frightful suffering was caused him by the ignorance and wantonness of others. They forced upon *him*, to whom even the smell of such things was the cause of terror, tobacco, and snuffs, and spirituous liquors, and placed him consequently in a condition even to frighten the savages themselves

on. When I had been a considerable time with the police, they brought me to the Tower. I was obliged to go up a very high hill and wept, as everything had done me great hurt. When I came to the Tower, one man spoke again so loud, that I felt still more pain: the same man made me go up another higher hill, that is, the staircase, he opened the door, which made a great noise, and then first could I take rest.* But I wept still a long time, until I became sleepy, as everything gave me pain; at last, however, I fell asleep; when I heard something at which I was so amazed, and I listened to it with such attention, as in my former situation I had never heard anything like it.† This attention I cannot indeed describe. I listened very long, but when, after some time, I heard nothing more, and my attention ceased,

---

who caused or allowed it. Even from the smell of brandy, which is always offensive to a man in such a case, when brought near him, he experienced pains in his head all day long, and from squeezed cheese, &c. pain in his stomach of equal duration.

This is according to Hauser's account heard by me in 1828, and compared by me with other intelligence. How he thrust away the plate with the beer and meat has been seen before.

* Such like sounds, which others heed not at all, attracted his attention.

† The striking of the Tower-clock, which awoke him, for he, as appears, by what follows, awoke in the night.

I felt a pain in my feet. I remarked that I felt no pain in my eyes, and I knew not why. It was not become day, which was of the greatest benefit to my eyes. But in other respects I felt pain in my whole body, especially in my feet.* I sat up, I wished to quench my thirst with the water that stood near me, for which I felt. I saw no more water and bread, instead of which I saw the floor, which had appeared quite different in my former dwelling place. I wished also to look about for my horses and play, but they were not there, whereupon I said, *I möcht ah*, &c., by which I meant to say, Where are my horses and the water and bread? Hereupon I remarked the sack of straw on which I sat. I examined it with great astonishment, and I knew not what it was. When I had considered it a very long time, I beat it with my fingers, by which means I heard the same sound as from the straw in my former dwelling place, on which I always used to sit and also sleep. I saw also many other things of which I fell into astonishment, and which cannot be described. I said, *I möcht ah*, &c., by which I meant to say, What is this there, and where are my horses?

* First also when he heard nothing more. Compare note (§) p. 170, on this subject.

I again heard the clock strike; I listened very long, but I heard it no more. I saw the stove, which was of a green colour,* and brightness proceeded from it. Upon this also I said the above mentioned words, which the man had taught me; by which I meant to say, that he must also give me such a beautiful shining thing. I said it several times, but I received nothing. I looked at it very long. I said once again the same words; by which I meant to say to the stove, that my horses should not be so long in coming. I had a notion that the horses were gone away. I also had the thought when the horses came, to say, They shall go away no more. This also would I have said, No more they shall leave the bread, otherwise they have nothing.† With so much speaking I felt great thirst, and as I no longer saw any water, I lay down and slept: when I awoke again, I felt again the same pain in my eyes as I had felt in my way towards the city.. When I awoke again it was day, and the brightness of day was very painful to

* He could, as has been remarked, at first distinguish colours in deep darkness.

† He was accustomed, as already mentioned, to feed his toy horses with the bread of which he ate himself. Here he warns them not to run away from their bread, that they might not want fodder.

me.* I began to cry, and said, *I möcht ah,* &c. *Dahi weis wo Brief hi ghörts;* by which I meant, Why is it that something does so much hurt to my eyes? He shall drive away this which occasions me so much pain in my eyes. Give me the horses quickly, and plague me not thus always.† I heard the same thing as I had heard at first, but I mean, however, that it was somewhat different, as I heard it much louder; it was not the same, but (instead) that the clock struck, it was become sounding.‡ This I listened to a very long while; but when from time to time I heard it continually less and less, and when my attention was at an end, I said these words, *Dahi weis wo Brief hi ghört,* by which I meant to say, he might also give me such a beautiful thing, and not always teaze me.§ I lay a long while; the man lifted me up no longer, I sat up by myself. I remarked that I was in the same place; then thought I likewise this, that I should feel no

* Even when I became acquainted with Hauser, his eyes appeared still somewhat inflamed.

† It is worthy of remark, that Hauser occasionally addressed an indefinite general person, by whom he thought that his pain was caused, in order to procur e assistance, and to get what he wanted.

‡ The word audible was wanting to him; thence his wonderful struggle with the expression.

§ Namely the striking of the clock, as it occurs often afterwards.

longer any pain in my eyes*, and hear the same thing. At length I stood up; I also set myself down again, as my feet gave me very great pain. I began to weep again, and said the words which I had learned, by which I meant, Why are the horses so long without coming, and let me suffer so much? I wept a very long time, and the man came no more. I heard the clock strike; this always took away half of my pain†, and on which the thought comforted me, that now the horses will soon come. And during this time, as I listened, a man came to me, and asked me all manner of things; perhaps I gave him no answer, as my attention was turned towards what I heard. He seized me by the chin, and lifted up my head, by which means I felt a frightful pain in my eyes from the day-light.‡ The man of whom I now speak, was he that was shut up with me,

* He remarked that he was in the same place in the Tower in which he found himself at his first waking in the night, and therefore thought, on his having felt no pain in his eyes at that time, that he was still on the road with his conductor, and expected that this man would, at his waking, raise him from the ground, as he had done on the way.

† As before, he first felt the pains no longer when he heard the clock, so they leave him here also when he hears it.

‡ That the man had first questioned him is the conjecture of Hauser.—Vide note (‡) p. 165. Hauser means to say, the man probably questioned me, and, as I gave him no answer, he caught me by the chin.

therefore I did not know that I was shut up. He began to speak to me; I listened to him a very long time, and constantly heard other words; then I said to him my words already mentioned, *Dahi weis wo*, &c.; by which I meant, What is that which has given me so much pain in my eyes when thou hast held up my head? But he had not understood me in what I said; he had well understood what the words signified, but not what I meant. He let my head go, seated himself near me, and continually asked me questions. In the meanwhile, the clock began to strike. I had my attention turned towards that the instant I heard it; I must long have listened to the man; he took me by the chin, turned my face towards him, and would again have asked me* what I listened to so attentively, but I understood him not in what he said. I said to him, *I möcht ah*, &c., by which I meant, that he should give me such a beautiful thing†; but he understood me not, as to what I meant to say; he continued to speak, however: I began to weep, and said, *Ross ham;* by which I meant to say, he shall not always plague me

* Instead of "he may have asked me," probably, he asked me.
† The sound of the clock, as once before already.—Vide note (§) p. 170.

so with speaking, all this gives me very great pain. He stood up, went away to where he lay, and left me to sit alone. I wept a very long while; I felt a great pain in my eyes, so that I could not weep any longer. I sat alone a very long time, then I heard something quite different, upon which I listened with such an attention as I cannot tell. What I heard was the trumpet in the Emperor's stable; but I heard not this long, and when I heard it no longer, I said, *Ross ham*—he shall also give me something so beautiful.* Then the man came to me here, and said several times the words which he had spoken before, very slowly at first, and I said after him; he said, Dost thou not know what this is?† I said these words to him several times, by which I meant to say, he shall give me the horses soon, and must not always plague me so. The man now stretched out his hand towards the water-pitcher, which stood under my bed, and wanted to drink, but I stretched out my hand towards it, and said, *Ross ham*. The man gave me the pitcher forthwith, and let me drink; when I had drank the water, I became so lively as cannot be described; I asked him for the

* The same tune as twice before, on hearing the striking and sound of the clock.

† It seems to be a blending of direct and indirect words.

horses. I said *Ross ham;* upon which he said several times, *I know not what thou wantest.* I said also the same words after him, but I could not immediately speak after him so clearly, and I said, *I wös net,* and by *Ross ham,* I meant to say, that he should also give me my horses. He understood not what I had desired, and stood up, went to the place where his bed was, and left me to sit alone. Just then the clock began to strike, which delighted me exceedingly, so that I always forgot my pain, and my longing was after this dwelling place.* Just then, *Hiltel,* the keeper of the prison, came, and brought the bread and water, which I knew again immediately, and said to it, *I möcht ah,* &c., by which I said to the bread, Now go not away again, and let me not be so plagued any more. He laid the bread down by me; I also took it up in my hand immediately; he poured the water into the pitcher, and set it down upon the floor. Just then he began to ask me questions. He questioned me with so harsh a voice, that it caused me much pain in my head, upon which I began to cry, and said, *I möcht ah,* &c. *I*

---

* It must be understood, *and I lost* the longing which I had after my former dwelling-place. I have already mentioned, that Hauser at first had a hankering after his cage where he had lived without pain.

wös net. In gross Dorfs da is die Voter.
These words I made use of without distinction
to get what I wanted. The keeper of the prison went out, as he had not understood me;
he knew the words well, as to what they
meant, but not what I had wished to express
by them, and I also understood not what he
had said to me. I ate my bread as soon as I
had brought it to my mouth; it was not so
hard as what I had eaten in my former dwelling-place.* I handled it, and saw that it still
was bread; it had the taste, but not the hardness.† I ate it, however, as I was hungry.
When I had had it a few minutes in my stomach, I felt great pain in my body. I began
to cry, and said, *Ham weisen*, by which I
meant to say, that he should not do us so
much injury, and might take me away to the
place where my horses were. Again I heard
the trumpet in the Emperor's stables. I listened, and was constantly delighted greatly, as
it was my hope, that when the horses come, I
tell them‡ what I have heard. I listened a

* His usual food was fine high-spiced rye-bread.

† In his place of confinement he had bread quite stale,
and therefore he could the less endure the newly-baked bread
which he had in the Tower.

‡ When Hauser expressed words and thoughts by himself,
in the earliest part of his residence in Nuremberg, he made
use of inaccurate modes of expression in what he said at that

very long time; I heard nothing more. Then came the keeper of the prison back again, and brought with him a piece of paper and a lead pencil. I knew this again immediately, at which I was so delighted that I cannot describe it, as I thought now I should soon receive my horses.* He gave me the paper and the lead pencil in my hand, and I wrote what he now had taught me, and this was my name, but I have not known what I have written. When I was ready with my writing, I said, *I möcht ah*, &c., by which I said, Now he shall give me the horses. He said, indeed, something, with a strong voice, which I have not understood, and took my paper and went out.

The Tenderness and Excellence of his Disposition at first.

The affecting image of the purest goodness which was vouched for by the appearance of Hauser at first, exceeds everything of this sort

time. Thus, he says, " I tell" with the suppression of " shall," or "will."

* In his dungeon, he had written with a pencil on paper, therefore he associated the sight of those objects with the idea of his horses which he had there, and meant, that as the former were at hand, the latter were not far off, as they were all connected together.

that can be devised by fancy; no description can express it in the fulness of its vivacity. There are the following proofs of this in the year 1828.

His peculiar sensibility, with respect to the external effects from all living creatures, being predominant, even those which do no hurt *to others*, could put him in a state of terror.

When, at one time, somebody desired him to inflict a slight blow on him with a little stick, he could not be induced to do it: he said that it would give much pain to himself. One man struck another before his eyes, and although the one who was struck assured him, laughing, that he felt no pain, still he could not remove from Hauser the terror and anguish which he felt at such a sight. When he saw some one really correcting a child, as it happened two or three times during his stay in the Tower, he shed tears, and became extremely uneasy.

About the time that he was entrusted to my care, I saw him fall into a paroxysm of anguish and displeasure, when some one caught up a cat by the neck in order to shew it to him. The fleas also in the Tower had caused him a great deal of annoyance, and with their bitings interrupted his sleep, but he was displeased when he saw them killed, and wished to put them out at the window. As somebody about that time killed a flea in his sight*, he left him with angry reproaches, and when the man said that this animal had been killed because it had plagued and bitten him, he said that it should have been put out of the window; but when it was remarked to him that then it might have leaped upon other men and have bitten them, he was in some degree tranquillized.

When any one was going to kill an insect, he hindered it, and said, This animal might also be very willing to live. When he saw a bird or other animals shut up, he was grieved, and said, This animal might also like to be at liberty, why is it shut up? I saw him weep when somebody said to him, in a joke, A certain cat was to be thrown to the snake which was then in Nuremberg. He was grieved even to tears when he heard that the horse on which he used to ride had a swollen leg; and when he was informed that this horse was going to represent a mule on the stage, he was angry, and said, that this brave nag ought not to be turned into ridicule. If he saw an animal

* With a shuddering he spoke afterwards of that " black thing." He was afraid of a hen in the same manner, and as it was of the same colour he regarded it on that account as just such a " black beast."

desirous of food, he insisted upon its being satisfied.

I was once obliged to set at liberty a fowl which was to have been roasted, in order not to excite his wrath. No one can have any notion of the affecting childishness with which he begged for it, and of the delight with which he saw it fly away.

With an expression of infinite sorrow he once said to me, " Mr. * * * has killed to day in his sporting, a hare and two birds, which I saw still bleeding. How is it possible (continued he) that men can have no pity for these animals, which have done no hurt to any one?" When he was told that men kill these animals in order to feed on their flesh, he replied, " A man might eat something else, bread for instance, as I did."

When in the autumn of 1828, he saw some monkeys which performed all kinds of feats, he took an infantine pleasure in the exhibition, but when he observed that they must re-commence them, in order to satisfy new spectators, with an expression of compassion he requested to be allowed to go out. He said afterwards that, through grief, he had not been able to look at them any longer, as he had experienced how contrary it is to the inclination of any one to be obliged to say and shew again and again what he has already said and shewn to curious persons a thousand times.

The first thing that he read, and probably understood (in the year 1828), was the history of Joseph and his Brethren. He had unspeakable pleasure in it, but complained exceedingly of the harshness with which Joseph treated his brethren in Egypt at first, and said that this was not right. In the situation of Joseph he would not have distressed his brethren, he would have forgiven them the wrong which they had done to him, as much as they needed it, and have let them go, but he would have kept with him Reuben who had saved his life.

Although hitherto quite without religious education, yea, wishing to know nothing at all of religion and christianity, yet he returns not evil for evil, but is willing to do good to those who had hated and plunged him into wretchedness. But how truly human, at the same time, is the remark made above by Hauser.— He is willing, indeed, to do no evil to those who have treated him so cruelly, but still he cannot love them: but Reuben, who has done good to him, whom he loves, he would keep with him.

One of his exquisite declarations which he made in October 1828, is the following:—He reflects also very unwillingly on his imprisonment, because he pictures to himself the anxiety in which the unknown, who kept him in confinement, must have lived. He has probably always desired his death, which has not taken place, and therefore he believes that the unknown, until he had released him, must have lived in the most tormenting disquietude, which gives him pain when he thinks of it. Such declarations from Hauser at that time were neither generally the consequence of education and moral improvement; nor, moreover, did they proceed from well-grounded religious influence: they flowed purely and spontaneously from their own source, so to speak, in his hitherto untroubled human nature, but which his life in the world soon compelled to fall away of themselves.

The assassination which was attempted upon him produced a very bad impression on his mind. He declared afterwards, that if the unknown who had held him in confinement, and whom he steadfastly maintained to be the very person that had attempted the murder, were discovered, he would beg for him, as, notwithstanding that, he had brought him up like a child, and had not killed him: but at present, he says, that if he were taken, men might do with him what they would.

A few weeks after he was wounded, exercising himself in shooting at a mark, and once hitting it very well, he came running into me rejoicing, and said, that now he could shoot a man. So altered then was that being who was previously so harmless, that he would not allow any small insect to suffer, even though it had hurt himself!

Dreams.

1. In my house Hauser slept for the first time in a regular bed, which pleased him uncommonly, when compared with the hardness of his former couch, although this pleasure was disturbed by a certain disagreeable sensation which the feathers powerfully caused.* On the first night which he passed in bed, he had his first dream, which was conjoined with this circumstance, namely, the malady under which he laboured at that time, was that night alleviated. The lady of the Burghermaster (Binder), for whom he had a very remarkable partiality, came to his bed, he said, and inquired of him how he found himself. To his answer, that his headache had not yet left him,

---

* This feeling was lost subsequently, but after the attempted assassination, by which he was brought back to his early nervous sensibility, sleeping in his accustomed feather bed occasioned him again an unpleasant sensation.

she replied, that he must only have patience, and soon it would be better; she stretched out her hand towards him, saluted him, and withdrew.* Hereupon something sank down from his head to the lower parts of his body, the pain in his head departed, and for joy he laughed excessively.† He now steadfastly affirms that the Burghermaster's lady went away that night with his headache. We endeavoured to convince him that the preceding was an illusion of the imagination, but in vain; he knew for certain, he said, the abovementioned lady had been by him, that he really had given her his hand, and that she had said to him, Adieu, Caspar! Also, when the lady came herself and confirmed the assertion of its being a dream, he did not believe it, and occasionally also expressed himself in terms of contradiction, in this manner, " he must surely believe what the Burghermaster's lady and the Burghermaster said; but still he knew for a certainty that she had been with him." However, at last, he appeared to be convinced. But as the lady asked him, at her departure,

---

* The affectionate treatment which he experienced in the Burghermaster's house had made an indelible impression upon him.

† Here is meant, that childish laugh of which mention has been made before.

if he would visit her that day, and if he did not feel himself still too weak to go out, he replied, that as the Burghermaster's lady had visited him the night before, he would also go to her. As he afterwards dreamt more frequently, he began to apprehend the nature of dreams. On the day which followed that beneficial night, the obstruction of his bowels was removed, and twice they were opened. The headache was gone, according to his dream. But the greatest nervous debility, difficulty of digestion, and a confined state of bowels, still continued for some time.

2. In the spring of 1829 he had the following dream:—A beautiful male figure approached his bed in white raiment, and reached out a garland to him, with this observation, that he must die in a fortnight. Hauser said to the figure, in reply, he had not yet been long in the world, and must not die yet; whereupon the former rejoined, that it would be better if he were to depart from the world without a long life. On this the man laid the garland on a table. Hauser stood up to take it; it gradually became brilliant, and as it grew brighter and glittered continually more and more, Hauser said, I will die, and soon after awoke. I bade him describe the dream, and he wrote what follows :—

"On the night of the 2nd of April, I had a dream, as if I had really seen a man; he had on a white cloth, which hung round his body, his hands and feet were bare, and he had appeared exceedingly beautiful.* Then he stretched out his hand to me with something that was like a garland; then he said I should take it; then I was willing to take it, then he gave me for answer, In a fortnight thou must die; then I gave him for an answer, I may not die yet, as I am not long in the world, and took not the garland; when he gave me for an answer, It is better to do so: then he stood before me a long time. As I took not the garland, he went back towards the table, and laid it down upon the table; as soon as he had laid it down upon the table, and as I came nearer, it had received a glorious brightness. Then I took it and went away to my bed; as I came nearer to the bed, it continually became brighter; then I said, I will die; then he went away. I was willing to stand up in my bed, then I became awake."

The garland, in the symbolical imagery of this dream, is evidently death; it is at first devoid of brilliancy, *id est*, it has no meaning

* Hauser made use of the pluperfect tense as the imperfect. In the same manner, farther on,—it had received a glorious brightness.

with regard to Hauser, who on that account wishes not to die; but the garland begins to be resplendent, and as it continually increases in brightness, it excites in Hauser a longing after death, and a higher view of it, and now he wishes to die.

Hauser's Visit to a Somnambulist.

In December 1829, Hauser, for certain reasons, was brought into contact with a female somnambulist, who was at that time at Nuremberg with her magnetic operator, Professor Hensler, from Munich. Hauser, by the proximity of this person, was seized with the greatest aversion; in the same manner, on the other hand, she experienced a peculiarly abhorrent effect from Hauser. I ordered him to put on paper an account of the sensation which he felt, which he did as follows: " As I came into the room, and the door of the deceased person was opened, which I did not know, I felt a sudden dragging on both sides of my breast, as if any one wished to pull me into the room; as I went in, and proceeded towards the sick person, a very strong breath blew on me, and as I had her at my back, it blew on me from behind, and the pulling which I felt before in my breast I now felt in my shoulders. As

I went towards the window, the sick person followed me. At the time that I wished to ask a question of Mr. Von Tucher, I felt a trembling in my left foot, and it became unwell; she went back again, and that trembling left me; she seated herself under the canopy, and said, Will not the gentleman sit down? Hereupon Mr. Professor Hensler said to her, she should see me; so as she drew nigh to me, within two or three steps, I was still more unwell than before, and I felt pains in all my limbs. Mr. Professor Hensler told her that I was the man who had been wounded *; at the same time she noticed my scar, and pointed towards it; then came the air strong upon my forehead, and I felt pain in it; also my left foot again began to tremble greatly. The sick person seated herself under the canopy, and said, that she was ill, and I also said that I was so unwell, that I must sit down; I sat down in the other room: now the other foot began to twitter. Although Mr. Von Tucher held my knees, I could not keep them still. Now a violent beating of my heart came on me, and there was a heat in all my body; that beating of my heart left me afterwards, and I had a twittering in my left arm, which ceased after some minutes, and I was again something

* That is, by the attempt which had been made to assassinate him.

better. This condition lasted until the next morning; then I had a headache again, and a twittering in all my limbs; still not so violent. In the afternoon, about three o'clock, it came again, something less, and left me earlier; my bowels were opened, and again in half an hour after, then I was quite well again."

The somnambulist was greatly affected by the presence of Hauser. I heard, that afterwards, when she was asleep, she had said these words, "That was a hard struggle for me." She felt indisposition from it, even the next day. I myself could not keep in the apartment of the somnambulist. A severe affection of the eyes, which abated when I entered the adjoining apartment, and increased again when I returned; and, lastly, a glow in my face, necessitated me to retire altogether. When on the following day I suffered myself to be induced to take the somnambulist by the hand, which I was soon obliged to relinquish, and when, by the order of the magnetic operator himself, she blew on me, I became feverish, and also felt the next day the most disagreeable excitation.

The Effect of a Spider.

In the year 1829, in the afternoon of the 9th of September, a spider let itself down from its web on Hauser's head: as it came on the upper part of his head, he felt a chill, and an excessive degree of cold in his forehead, without knowing the cause. As it proceeded farther down, he put up his hand, and crushed the spider on his under lip; hereupon he felt, for more than a quarter of an hour, a burning pain, which past away with a tremor. On his going to bed the burning sensation returned. In the night the part swelled, and there rose on it several small bladders, out of which there was a discharge of white pus in the morning, and on the following night several bladders appeared again near that part. On the evening of the 26th of August, as he was reading, a cold tremor came over him, similar to that produced by the snake. He looked round, and perceived nothing, but he became colder and colder, and on closer examination he discovered, not far distant, a large spider creeping down the wall. He took a light in order to have a view of it, and with his right hand, which was previously in a bad state, in consequence of a fall from the bar at the gymnastic school. As he put it close to the spider, so great a pain siezed him in that arm, that he was obliged to let the light fall. In order to alleviate the pain, he put his finger close to the remaining bottle of lotion which he had previously used for that hurt. He felt a pain downwards from above; then the sensation went back to the shoulder, then from that part to the feet, and back again. After some minutes, all the pain left him. But the chill which had been occasioned by the spider, was of long continuance. His right arm, which had been so violently affected by being approximated to the spider, appears at that time to have been somewhat more susceptible of such effects than usual, in consequence of the hurt just mentioned.

The Effect of a Flower; written by Hauser himself.

"I went into Mr. Haubenstricker's garden and found a flower which has pleased me very much. I looked at it a long time, and considered it well—then I asked Mr. Haubenstricker what sort of a flower this was. He gave me for answer, 'A crown imperial.' The next morning I told Mr. Professor, that I had seen a very fine flower, and related to him how it looked; then said Mr. Professor, that I should bring one. I went into the garden and laid hold of one; as I siezed it and wished to pluck it off, the very same feeling came upon me, as from the serpent, which I have seen. I felt a chill; after some time I grew very hot, and felt a head-ache for a quarter of an hour, and my hand in which I held the flower was as if it were lame. This lasted five minutes. Before the head-ache went away, a shivering came over me, then thos feelings went away, but for some hours I was not so well as before. I became very weary; and so it also happened in consequence of the serpent."*

Intoxication by means of Grapes.

Enjoyment from grapes and fresh grape juice occasioned in Hauser a state of elevation, heat, and intoxication, even to such a degree that he was obliged to remove his inebriety by sleep. After he had once tasted a grape, and I myself had seen the effect of it, I forbade him immediately to eat grapes; still, to please himself, once in September 1828, he tasted two or three drops of newly made wine, and immediately he exhibited the perfect image of a drunken man. He staggered, spoke with difficulty, and laughed incessantly, at the same time he extolled the taste of the juice; the little finger of his left hand was in strong motion, as was usually the case in violent excitements, and soon after he was obliged to throw himself on the bed. Thus

* Respecting the effect of the serpent (a rattle-snake), to which Hauser alludes here, vide ante, page 110, where it was given in consequence of my information.

the fruit of the vine, just as it came out from the hands of nature, developed in him those symptoms which in others are only the effect of the fermented liquor. Heat flew up in his head from green grapes, but not from purple ones. A sensation of something running down in his hands and feet, that he experienced after much enjoyment, was also felt by him in this instance. He himself wrote the following:—

"Sept. 9, 1828.

"On Wednesday evening I ate some juice of purple grapes, and I scarcely had it in my body two minutes before I felt a violent giddiness, so that I no longer knew any letter in a book, no more could I read, and I was obliged to lie down and go to sleep. I only took a tea-spoonful."

"Sept. 5, 1829.

"* * * *—He gave me a grape from a bunch, I ate it. Immediately a slight heat arose in my head. After this I became very light in my head, also (I felt) a little giddiness, and there ran from it a very strange feeling into my arms and feet, as if somebody had thrown water upon me; that running down reached as far as the tips of my fingers (and also of my toes)."

The addition between parenthesis is supplied

by me. Between both events there is an interval of a year; therefore the second, by the greatly diminished weakness and sensibility, shews the proportionate difference.

CONJECTURES

Respecting Caspar Hauser's Place of Confinement, &c.

BY M. SCHMIDT VON LÜBEC.

I. *The dwelling-place of the unknown, and also the place of confinement of Hauser is in the neighbourhood of Nuremberg, three or four miles distant at most.*—Although in the investigation, the public attention has been particularly directed towards the distant districts of Bavaria, namely, the Upper and Lower Danube, also the circle of Regen and Iser, yet there is the greater ground for the above conclusion. That the unknown's place of residence is in Nuremberg itself, is not to be supposed, as in that case he would at least have known the name of the captain of the horse, to whom he sent Hauser, which it appears he did not, as he simply addressed the letter to the well-born Captain. Also Hauser's own declaration, and especially the circumstance that his feet were bloody, and that the soles of his feet were stripped of the epidermis, sufficiently prove that he came into the city after a journey on foot; still, however, it does not appear that he came from a great distance. The following are the grounds upon which we are induced to hold this opinion. The unknown is desirous of releasing Caspar Hauser from his late confinement, and of placing him in a regiment of horse. For that purpose he chooses the regiment or squadron which is stationed at Nuremberg. There seems scarcely to have been any particular reason for this choice, as he does not once mention the name of the captain; the chief cause for this choice, was, as it seems, the proximity of the place. That regiment of horse was nearest to his residence. The proximity must certainly have been the most powerful reason on many accounts. There was clearly considerable difficulty, and also the greatest danger in bringing from a great distance, a youth who was unable to walk; and in this place also, immediately in the neighbourhood of his own residence, he might easily keep him in sight and watch his steps: and, at all events, if the affair did not proceed according to his wishes, he might take him back. The objection may be made:—How did the unknown dare venture to leave Hauser in the neighbourhood? How easily the latter might meet him once again accidently, and recognize him! We reply, that the fear of being known again by Hauser after some time, could not be very great: that Hauser probably would not be able to recognize him after a month had elapsed, especially in another dress different from that in which he had seen him, as he could not have had any distinct impression of him, through a want of a comparison with the countenances of others, and that of the unknown; and that the unknown during his confinement and by means of his own pre-arrangement might have provided against that occurrence. But even supposing the worst: granting that Hauser had once met and distinctly recognized him, what then could the unknown have had to fear? Hauser was not even aware of his guilt: the unknown might fearlessly have appeared before him, and claimed his gratitude for the care taken of him during sixteen years, as well as for having placed him in the king's service in the cavalry; for, had he been received by the cavalry, as was expected, without further inquiry into the affair, Hauser would have known nothing of any other connexion with him. Only let not what then was the case be exchanged for what followed, when Hauser, contrary to all the expectations of the unknown, was made acquainted with the bad treatment which he had experienced. If the unknown had entertained the least suspicion that the affair would have taken such a course as it has, he most assuredly would not have brought Hauser to Nuremberg.

It will be farther objected with respect to the proximity of Nuremberg, that Casper Hauser himself has declared that he spent two or three days in his journey. Declared? Yes, as well as anything can be considered a declaration by such a neglected youth, who knows scarcely fifty unconnected words, not understanding the meaning of one of them, and who, of all the objects between heaven and earth, has, in truth, heard, seen, and perceived nothing. What is called his declaration is nothing more than what the Burghermaster (Binder) at Nuremberg, has made out at random, from some words and signs when he was interrogated. Not to misunderstand the proper meaning of the question, and to see the true connexion of the business, was, under such circumstances, almost an impossibility. But for once we will assume the case that the Burghermaster (Binder) has judged correctly respecting what Hauser wished to say, and also Hauser has rightly comprehended the questions which were put to him: in short, we will admit that Hauser has really spent two or three days in coming from his place of confinement to Nuremberg; what has that to do with the distance? No idea of the length of way can be formed by a wretched being who had not learned to walk, but only how to creep. The unknown, also, certainly did not take him by the direct road; but brought him by solitary, cross, and bye-ways, and made frequent haltings; also let it be admitted that in the dark he carried him on his back a few hundred paces, yet, for all that we do not believe that it could have been possible for him to take the young man more than a mile a day. The circumstance that the unknown is very well acquainted with the city and its environs, tends further to prove the proximity of Caspar's residence to Nuremberg. He knows the Neumark (New-market); he knows Neuthorstrasse (New-gate-street), and that the Captain of the horse lives there, for Hauser enquired for Neuthorstrasse, of the citizen whom he met with in Unschlitt plasse (or Unschlitt place). He is also, as it is probable, the man who attempted the murder on the 17th of October, 1829; this also proves the nearness of his dwelling; for he must be frequently in the city to look out for a seasonable opportunity, and he must also be acquainted with the situation of Professor Daumer's residence.

11. *The unknown speaks the ancient dialect of Bavaria.*—Caspar Hauser spoke that dia-

lect. For as he had heard and seen no other man during a long series of years except him, so necessarily he must have learned the dialect from him; but by no means does it follow that the unknown has also dwelt among the old Bavarians; only that he drew his origin from the place where they dwell.

III. *The unknown is probably of the Catholic religion.*—His presumptive descent from the old Bavarians, speaks in favour of this supposition. It is farther corroborated by the rosary and the Catholic prayer books which he gave to Hauser. It is true, that the rosary and prayer books may have been given with a view to mislead, and to gain belief to the assurance, that he was from the confines of Bavaria. But we can scarcely give credit for such a finesse, to a man whom we have learned to know by means of his letter, which has been mentioned before. If craft and subtlety had been played off here, he would also have gone a step farther. He would have made mention of religion in his letter, or in the postscript, and would have searched for some prayer books in the pure Bavarian dialect; instead of which, the prayer books are in part, from Prague and Salzburg, and of ancient date, and appear to have lain for many years in a spiritual armoury, and now to have been taken out at random.

In addition to this, a man is never in the habit of sporting with religion without the most urgent necessity, which could not by any means have been the case here; but it is not a necessary consequence of this, that Caspar Hauser must have derived his origin from Catholic progenitors. There is, indeed, no probability afforded to us either for or against this.

IV. *The unknown is no day-labourer, as he asserts, but belongs to the half-educated middling class.*—A poor day-labourer may, indeed, in early youth, have learned to write, and perchance, also, in German and Roman letters at the same time; but to write a letter in a scholar-like manner, similar to what is before us, is not likely. First, the full title, according to the requirement of the rank: "well-born," "exceedingly well-born;" "excellent Mr. Captain;" then the proper superscription, "from the Bavarian confines," &c. &c. then the most appropriate subscription *in optima forma;* lastly, "the postscript." A poor day-labourer, who with ten children has nothing to live on, with difficulty even inhabits a house that is sufficiently commodious to conceal in it, from all the world, a young man during sixteen years; he seldom inhabits it for so long a course of years without changing.

Also, no one entrusts a child to a poor day-labourer for the purpose of education. Even the sportive wit in the name *Hauser*, which means that he never proceeded from the house, indicates a species of education which is wont to be peculiar to the middle rank.

V. *The unknown had also to arrange a particular locality in which he might conceal his prisoner with security during so many years.*—It is not easy to imagine such a long concealment in his own house. In that case he must have inhabited it alone. In addition to this locality, he must have had to make such an arrangement as to have the whole time of *Hauser's imprisonment* without interruption. Yes, even from the first moment of *Hauser's* confinement, he must have depended on a long and secure use of this place thenceforward, as by a change of residence the danger of detection would have been too great; and where, then, in the new dwelling would there have been a secret place of confinement?

VI. *The place in which Hauser was confined, must not lie in any part completely solitary.*—This was shewn partly by the anxiety observable in the watch over him, and partly by the circumstance that the unknown deemed it necessary to convey him away by night.

VII. If the declaration of Hauser can be relied on, that the unknown only came every fifth day, or after a certain number of days, for the purpose of instructing him, it must thence be concluded, that the same man had an appointed service himself, which was the cause of his absence during a certain number of days.

VIII. *Hauser's food was the usual prison fare, coarse bread and water.*—This kind of sustenance cannot have been by chance, because it was entirely without exception; but as little as the other circumstances can this be attributed to great indigence. Potatoes and other kinds of food are, in fact, just as cheap, and no poverty is so great as not to admit of finding out means for a difference of food occasionally, during so long a series of years. The ten children of the unknown have not always and constantly been kept on nothing but coarse bread and water. No particular motive, as far as one can conjecture, seems likely to have been the cause of this strict diet. At most, it can only have been the suggestion of the cloister. But some may have been led, both by means of the prison fare, and by the circumstances mentioned above, to conclude, that it was the regular fare of a prison establishment, where many might be fed on water and bread, and where this fare might be given to the prisoners in the cheapest, most secret, and unobserved manner. If this conjecture be not admitted, Hauser's mode of sustenance remains the most incomprehensible expedient of the whole history itself. Or the notion may be entertained, that at first there was no intention of effecting his death immediately, but that it was much more desirable that he should die gradually; and that, after this idea had been relinquished, Hauser had become so accustomed to his late food that he wished to have nothing besides.

IX. *A conjecture, or if that is too much, a suspicion forces itself on us, that the unknown was formerly a military man.*—Several circumstances induce us to form such an opinion. The style of the letter, the horses which he gave to Hauser as play things, the wish to place him in the cavalry, his acquaintance with the military station at Nuremberg, the appropriate titles given to the commander, and, lastly, the dress which he gave him on the way —boots with horse shoes, and the soles nailed, pantaloons trimmed between the legs, gilt loops, which were fashionable some years since. This dress could not have been bought second hand, as that was too dangerous an expedient, but must have been taken by the unknown from his own wardrobe of cast-off clothes.

X. *The unknown is probably the murderer*

of the 17*th of October*, 1829.—It is, indeed, easy to be imagined that another wicked person, interested in Hauser's fate, and dissatisfied with the release itself, or anxiously fearful respecting the turn of events and the course of the inquiry, should resolve upon the murder; but, however, it is still more probable that the murderer was the unknown person himself. It will be obvious that he had no one privy to the secret at last, and that in the course of time, he trusted that the thread of the original romance of Hauser would have been broken; hence also it might be evident why the rewards which were offered in order to lead to a discovery of the assassin, were ineffectual. It has been asked, what, at that time, could induce the unknown to attempt the murder at the risk of his own life, as he had the young man so long in his power, and might then easily and securely have removed him; but instead of this he brought him to Nuremberg with fatigue and danger? The answer is not difficult; the unknown, at first, did not wish to kill the youth, but to place him in the cavalry, with the expectation that this would have happened without further consequences, and that the affair would have there ended; but unexpectedly it turned out differently. The commander of the regiment would not admit him, and consigned him to the magistrate, who took up the business seriously, and a strict inquiry was instituted: it became a public story, and the deed was regarded as an act of villainy in the highest degree deserving of punishment. Thus apprehensions of detection were excited in the unknown; and every recollection, every declaration of Hauser, might bring destruction on him; and any accidental meeting with him and recognition, might become the cause of alarm. The whole state of things became totally different also from what it was a few days before. It is also possible, that, in the summer of 1829, a trace was actually almost discovered, but however without its being found out; and that upon this it was determined by the unknown to delay his purpose no longer. It is easy, therefore, to conjecture, that from his hiding place he had watched the whole progress of the inquiry, and that he had not remained unacquainted with any particular respecting the history of the foundling through ignorance of the conversation of the day. It might be more difficult to answer another question, namely this: why the murderer wished to kill the youth by means of cutting, and not stabbing. A dagger or a knife is of easier concealment about the person, is easier to be in readiness for the deed, and effects its purpose more easily than a weapon which is designed for cutting, and which could only be used with success if the young man were without any covering on his head. One reason, it is true, may be admitted for the wound in the head, but it is too remote, and is too conjectural to allow any one to give credit to the unknown for such an expedient; namely, that if the cut-wound in the head did not deprive the youth of his life, it might at least deprive him of his reason and the power of thinking, and that was sufficient to answer his purpose. But, as we have said before, such reasoning seems not suitable to the person in question. The following explanation is much more simple, and therefore more probable. The unknown took that weapon which he had in his possession previously. He could not presume either to buy or borrow another for that purpose, as by that means he might be easily detected, as soon as publicity was given to the affair. Also, he was probably more habituated to cutting than to stabbing. And if our suspicion above, that the unknown was formerly in the military service, were more than mere suspicion, that would immediately afford sufficient reason for the cut.

With the commencement of the year 1832,

we may date a new epoch in the life of Hauser. The city of Nuremberg, that had publicly declared him to be her adopted son, with the addition that she would deliver him up to no one who could not bring forward proof of legitimate claim to him, has found herself induced, however, to resign her adopted son as a foster-son to a British peer (Lord Stanhope). This Lord Stanhope, the son of the celebrated parliamentary orator, Charles Stanhope, who died the first of December, 1816, and sister's son of the prime minster Pitt, has had him since January at Anspach, and there in the mean time has placed him under the care of a proper tutor, until he proceeds with him to England. Respecting the cause, and the more immediate circumstances of this occurrence, hitherto nothing is known to us. According to Feuerbach's account, in page 139 above, the only passage in it, except the dedication, in which the business is mentioned, Lord Stanhope has adopted him through generosity, in order to relieve him from an improper mode of treatment at Nuremberg. It cannot be wholly denied that not only in making the investigation on the part of the city police, but also in the kind of treatment which Hauser experienced, corporeally and mentally, there is much that deserves commiseration. The continued inclination to brood over his destiny, of which Caspar must be daily reminded at Nuremberg, being removed he will begin a new life; as soon as the sails are spread to convey him to England, all melancholy reflections will be left behind him. New air, new modes of life, and new interests of life, will restore freshness and strength to his youth. Probably there is reserved for him in England a quiet, and therefore a more certain happiness, than he (even if he belonged to a race of princes) might have found on the tempestuous sea of time, if the hand of wickedness had not made him such an *incognito*; therefore we will not pity his fate any longer. From his experience hitherto, his confidence in the human race must rather assume bright than gloomy colours. For two or three wretches, who not out of hatred, but from sefish views, did him wrong, he has found hundreds who do him good, without any regard to their own interests. As long as he lives, then, he will reflect with love and gratitude on the men who have, in his forlorn condition, so paternally espoused his cause.

Finally, we cannot deny ourselves the wish and hope, that the inquiry respecting the mystery may be prosecuted in the absence of the youth. If, also, in order *to reach the giant perpetrator, it will be necessary to fight with the high and mighty Colossuses that keep guard before the golden castle gates,* still there are side ways to penetrate to him. But even if we were deprived of all means of finding any solution of the mystery respecting the former confinement of Hauser and the unknown person, still it would not appear to me that all hope would be lost; if all were to fail, we trust to an Almighty providence, to which no distance is too distant, and no height is too high, and no abyss too deep.

Conclusion. Assassination of Caspar Hauser, and discovery of a clue to the Mystery of his Birth.

THE short life of Caspar Hauser was terminated on the 17th of December 1833, by the dagger of an unknown assassin; though there is little room to doubt that it was the same individual who made an unsuccessful attempt in the October of 1829. The following statement of the particulars of his death are given in the German papers:

Caspar lived at Anspach, and Lord Stanhope during his stay there, had provided for his support. The president of the Court of Appeal had also given him employment in the Registrar Office. On his return from the Courts at mid-day, he was accosted in the streets by a person who promised to impart to him some highly important communications, and he appointed a meeting in the Castle Park. Instead of informing his friends of the circumstance, Hauser remained silent, and went about three o'clock to the place of assignation. The stranger, who was waiting for him, took him aside, and suddenly with a dagger inflicted upon him a mortal wound. In half an hour after he left his home, Hauser returned, almost breathless, and rushed into the apartment of his tutor, but was only able to utter at intervals, the words, "Parc—bourse—Uz—monument," and almost immediately fainted; it was not till then that his tutor discovered that he was wounded. He promptly sent a soldier of the police to the Castle Park, who found no one, but near the monument of the poet Uz, he picked up a small lady's work-bag, made of violet-coloured silk, containing a paper, on which was written the following words, but so crossed that it was found neccessary to hold it up to the window to read them:

"Hauser will be able to tell very distinctly how I have acted and whence I came. To save Hauser the trouble I tell you myself whence I came; I come from the Bavarian frontier . . . .

upon the river of ...... I will tell you even more, the name, M. I. O."

Hauser was struck with terror, and was able to give to the police only a few particulars of the description of the assassin.

Thus has terminated the existence of a man whose life and death have been equally unfortunate.

The history of Hauser is one of the most singular events of our time, and perhaps more mysterious than that of the man with the iron mask. It might be conceived that the policy of a despot might have an interest in the concealment of an important personage; but what interest could it have in bringing up in complete isolation an infant—in making it a prisoner, during the whole of its infancy, in the hands of a gaoler, and afterwards abandoning it to public charity—and, finally, to cause its assassination? How can there exist, in our age, a monster capable of such a refinement of cruelty?

What is scarcely less strange is that the Bavarian police, which is so vigilant on other, perhaps less important, occasions, has not been yet able to discover the least trace of the wretches who have several times attempted the life of this poor young man, and who have at last accomplished their abominable purpose.

The chief Burghermaster of Nuremberg has caused to be inserted in the journals of Bavaria the following notice, on the subject of this catastrophe:—

"Caspar Hauser, my dear pupil, is no more. He died yesterday, at ten o'clock at night, at Anspach, from a wound which he received from an assassin. The problems which Providence had attached to his melancholy existence are now solved for this victim of the horrible barbarity of his relatives. God, in his justice, will compensate him with an eternal spring of the joys of infancy, which were denied to him, for the vigour of youth of which he was deprived, for the life which has been destroyed only five years after it had begun to be acquainted with human society. Peace to his ashes.

"BINDER, Chief Burghermaster."
"*Nuremberg, Dec.* 18."

The mystery of the birth of Caspar Hauser is now, we also learn, in a fair way of being elucidated, and the Conjectures of Schmidt von Lübec, as given in the Appendix, will be found to be well grounded. Caspar Hauser is said to be "the product of an illicit amour; that a Priest, the reputed father, took charge of the child from the moment of its birth, and finally inclosed it in a subterraneous hole or vault in a convent where he was residing; that thus imprisoned and shut out from all human intercourse, the unhappy being passed his existence until within a day or two of his being found as related in the History, when the priest, being compelled to quit the convent, and having no other place of concealment at hand, released and left the boy to his fate." * * * " The chain of circumstantial evidence by which thus much of the story has been made out, is so well put together as to leave little doubt that the true elucidation has been hit upon."

The individual who first discovered this mystery is still pursuing his inquiries; and when he has thoroughly sifted the matter, should he favour the world with a Memoir on the subject; we shall take the necessary measures for ensuring an early translation of it for the English public.

Printed in the United Kingdom
by Lightning Source UK Ltd.
123258UK00002B/160/A